To Love and Cherish

by the same author

Black Diamonds, Yellow Apples
Once Round the Umbrella Tree

ELSIE GADSBY

To Love and Cherish

A Wartime Marriage

Illustrated by
ELLIE CHAMBERLAIN

BBC Radio Derby/
Derbyshire County Council's
Library Service

Co-published by
BBC Radio Derby, PO Box 269, Derby DE1 3HL
and Derbyshire County Council's Library Service

Copyright © Elsie Gadsby, 1988

First Published 1988

ISBN 0 903463 28 8

Illustrations by
Ellie Chamberlain
Walnut Cottage, Church Lane,
Maplebeck, Newark, Notts

Produced for the publishers by
Ashgrove Press, Bath BA1 3JN

Photoset by Ann Buchan (Typesetters),
Middlesex
Printed by Hillman Printers,
Frome, Somerset

To Love and Cherish

Chapter One

August 1940 was a hell of a time in which to get married. The Battle of Britain, which had started in earnest on July 10th, with air raids over the Channel, was well under way; and it was deemed best for civilians to keep away from coastal areas. In short, that meant holidaymakers. So bang went any idea that John and I had about a honeymoon.

August 3rd. A blazing hot day, and the wedding had gone well. Utility though it was. Borrowed wedding dress and veil; a rather frugal tea at my home. Frugal because of food rationing. But we DID have a wedding cake, with our family's pooled coupons, and a bottle of sherry and red wine.

After tea, John and I said goodbye to my Mam and Dad, and set off for the terraced house where we were to live with his Dad. But I could see our Mam looked a bit 'full up', the unaccustomed tears not far from her eyes; and Dad kissed me, (most unusual) and said, 'God bless ya' me' gel' or did he say 'God save ya'? Save me? From what? Oh heck, thought I, what unknown terrors lie in front of me? For this was 1940, remember, and the mysteries of sex still very much a closed book. No use asking our Mam about THINGS. She was too shy and non-forthcoming about THAT. So – this gel' would have to find out the hard way.

At the house on Slade Street where John lived; where we would both now live, two of his brothers and their wives, and four sisters and their husbands, also John's Dad, were waiting for us. They had brought bottles of beer AND a good thirst, and for the next three hours there was enough noise and laughter to split the old oak beams of the small living room. More beer was fetched from the Erewash pub, the laughter and jokes got coarser, and I began to feel a bit sick – and fed up, for I was a sensitive creature. Oh – if only we could have gone away, just for a few days. Curse Hitler – curse the War.

Then, an Uncle and cousin of John's arrived from Wirksworth; were surprised to find wedding celebrations in progress, and asked if they could stay the night. More beer was sent for; speech was becoming distinctly blurred.

'Don't drink too much John, will you?' I beseeched.

' 'Course not Elsie,' then, in an undertone, 'I wish they'd all go home.' He echoed my sentiment.

At last, at 10.30 they began to drift away, making unsteady progress up the street.

'I'll have to find something to cover over them from Wirksworth', I told John. 'For the bed. They'll have to manage with old coats.'

Fortunately there was an old iron bedstead, with a straw mattress in one of the two back bedrooms. John's Dad used the other room. I did the necessary improvisation, and the uncle and son made their unsteady, beery way upstairs, with just a candle to light their way.

Back in the living room one of the sisters was trying to rouse her husband from a drunken stupor on the sofa.

'I told him not to get too much – he can't tek' it,' then, after another almighty heave, 'Oh bugger 'im – he mun' stop there all nay'ht.' And off she went with the others.

I felt near to tears. My wedding night. Every girl's dream of her first step into the unknown realms of wedded bliss, and here I was in a strange house, with an old man in one bedroom, and two others I'd never even heard of before in another and now a brother-in-law in a drunken stupor in the living room. I felt like running back home. What a way to spend a wedding night, and I have never, not even these forty odd years afterwards forgotten the revulsion I felt. I was bitterly disappointed at what I thought was a poor start to this marriage we had so looked forward to.

I was awake first next morning; came down to make a pot

of tea, and found the errant brother-in-law wakening from his heavy sleep. He was very sorry for his behaviour.

'D'you want some breakfast?' I asked. He shook his head. 'A cup of tea then?' He accepted with lowered eyes, AND voice. He looked awful, and I felt a momentary feeling of pity, then – 'serve the daft thing right' I thought.

The others came down, one by one, and I had the unaccustomed task of making our meagre rations of bacon and eggs stretch to the limit. At home Our Dad had always fried the bacon and tomatoes, for breakfast on Sundays. I managed, but felt awfully shy with my new husband looking on, and aware of the knowing looks between the pair from Wirksworth.

The day passed, me being near to tears several times – especially when two of the brothers called and wanted John to go for a Sunday dinner-time drink, and I was left with just the old man for company. But thankfully my husband came home sober, and after dinner suggested a walk to the cemetery, to put my sheaf of lilies on his Mam's grave. She had died several years previously, before I had met John. It was lovely for us to be by ourselves for this brief hour; for I knew this would be impossible back at my new home – the old man never moved far from the house.

Back home I started to lay one of my new cloths over the old, wooden-topped table, in preparation for tea. The old man whistled pointedly, then he said,

'We never hae' a cloth on't table.'

'No? Well we've got one on now.' I answered sweetly. I started to cut the bread, thinly, and spread margarine on afterwards. Again that meaningful whistle.

'John d'unt like his bread as thin as that, an' I allus' put marg on f'ost.' He told me.

I was beginning to feel a bit peeved.

'Look here Dad,' I told him, 'If I'm going to see to things now I've got to do it my way – alright?' He merely shrugged, then started that whistle again.

It was the same when I attempted to stoke up the coal fire.

'It'll never bon' if ya' put t'coal on like that,' he told me. So I left that chore to him after that.

On our way to see Our Mam and Dad after tea I confided to my new husband,

'I don't think me and your Dad are going to get on very well.'

'You'll be alright in a bit,' he soothed. But I felt differently.

'John,' I hesitated, 'What do you say if we look at those new houses just past th'hospital? We'd be a lot better on our own.'

Several pairs of semi-detached houses were being built. The price? £350. Unbelievable isn't it – but true. Behind the houses fields stretched for miles, away up to the Shipley estate.

But we knew we'd never be able to afford one – we hadn't a spare penny between us, and we were afraid to take out a mortgage because of the possibility of John being called up for Military Service. He was a spare crane driver on the concrete pipe section at Stanton, and classed in an exempted category. But it was too risky. He just COULD be called up.

Air attacks by the Luftwaffe were getting stronger, especially around the coast. It was reported that 200 enemy planes had been sent to bomb London. In this battle alone we lost 19 planes and the enemy 28. It was at this time that Churchill told the British people,

'Never in the field of human conflict was so much owed by so many to so few.' And he was boosting the morale of us all wherever he went with his famous 'V' sign. As I said before, what a hell of a time in which to get married.

When we arrived at Mam and Dad's I felt terribly self-conscious. Mam was trying desperately hard not to look me full in the eyes, aware that I'd now no longer be a virgin, and I fully aware of my married status. Dad merely said,

'A-a-arta' alright me' gel.' He stuttered badly, an affliction which ran through the family, but which endeared him more than ever to me. I have always been profoundly aware of anyone afflicted, either mentally or physically, and feel a deep sense of pity for them, and am determined to help whenever I can. I thank God eternally that he bestowed a healthy body and mind on me, and for the gifts which I have made full use of.

I felt a great sadness when I again said 'Goodbye' to Mam and Dad, and selfconsciously walked back to my new home on my husband's arm. Several of my former neighbours stopped to wish us:

'Good luck to ya' both. Hope this bloody war d'unt last long.'

I fervently hoped not, for I didn't want to wait too long before starting a family, but didn't want us all to be blown to smithereens before that happy day dawned.

What a hell of a time in which to get married.

Chapter Two

During the months which followed, our War-time marriage settled down into an uneasy sort of routine; uneasy because of the threat of air raids, for the sirens continually sounded, and Air Raid Drill was carried out at all the large works and factories. We never went anywhere without our tin containing our gas masks. It was suicide to do so.

At the factory where I worked as a silk winder, I was allowed back on part-time. Single girls were on full time.

I knew I'd have to face the barrage of questions, innuendos, and nudge-nudge, wink-wink of the older married women about my newly married status.

I tried to adopt an air of amused detachment. But I secretly vowed they weren't going to get anything out of me. Besides, to me, the sexual side of marriage was, and always has been, sacred – a secret between man and wife. Now it's discussed and dissected in all the women's magazines isn't it – in Group Therapy Sessions, and by Marriage Guidance Counsellors.

Up till my wedding I had been an Ambulance Attendant at an Air Raid Post at Cotmanhay. Now I'd have to transfer to Chaucer Street Post, in the centre of town. Another set of people to get to know, another change in my life style.

There were my new neighbours to get to know too. The back door of our terraced house was in an entry leading to the rear of the houses, and used by the other residents. Not much privacy there I was to find out.

The old wash-house, sunken below yard level and minus window glass and door, and with the tiled roof caving in was shared by three families. It contained a copper, with fire hole underneath, a mangle and wooden ponch tub belonging to one of the women, and a zinc tub and dolly owned by the other woman. When it rained there'd be a puddle of water several inches deep to wade through. I used the copper to boil sheets and towels, but did the rest of my washing in the living room, in my new Ewbank washer. It was wallowed around entirely by hand, as was the wringer above. At my old home we'd got our own wash-house with a cold water tap. I'd never get used to this shared method, I was sure. But we did have separate flush lavatories, thank heavens.

I began to enjoy being a housewife, making the Sunday joint of shoulder lamb, or top side round stretch to its full limit; roasted on Sunday, cold on Monday, stewed on Tuesday, and using any bones left for broth on Wednesday. I had learned a lot about thrift off our Mam, and off Mrs Jackson in the short time I was 'out service'.

I began to make different cakes and tarts, and my Cornish pasties were a real treat. At least, that's what the Rev Money said one day when he called, to see how I was settling down to married life. He was the much loved Vicar of Trinity Church, and I'd given him one of the pasties for his tea.

Of course, with all the rationing I had to improvise, using egg powder, and dried, powdered milk. I tried making chocolate with powdered milk, crushed cornflakes and flavouring essence, and sometimes rolled around dates.

They were JUST eatable. Those of us with a really sweet tooth would have to wait until after the War to indulge ourselves.

John and I still went dancing occasionally, but mostly now went more often to the pictures, and on Saturday evenings, for a drink to the Durham Ox, or the Poplar on Bath Street. But sometimes he would be on night duty with the Home Guards at Stanton.

Often Sundays he would spend on manoeuvres, sometimes as far away as Alfreton.

One Sunday John came home looking agitated.

'What's up?' I asked. His face was a funny greenish, white colour.

'I was on guard duty, with fixed bayonet. We'd had word there might be 'Jerries' about, landin' wi' parachutes. Well – I heard this sound, coming from a dark entry. . .'

'Yes?' I was eager to hear more.

'Then I shouted "who goes there?" No answer – just this shuffling noise. "Stop or I fire". Still no answer. Then this dark figure came towards me and I just lunged out wi' mi' bayonet.'

'What happened then?' I gasped. He looked terrible.

'It were one o' our silly buggers weren't it – trying to catch us off guard. Well – I nicked his arm, an' it didn't half bleed.'

Of course there was an inquiry into the incident, but after that John was known as the first man who drew blood in the Stanton Home Guard.

Summer dragged on into Autumn. Every day there were accounts on the wireless of air raids over the big cities, with a particularly heavy blitz on October 11th over Liverpool with the loss of many lives.

On November 9th, 1940, it was announced that Neville Chamberlain, our former Prime Minister who had fought so hard for peace, had died.

That same month there were heavy bombings over Coventry, Birmingham, Southampton, Bristol and Liverpool, with the loss of 4,500 lives, and more than 6,000 seriously hurt.

Then on the 26th of November we learned of the creation of a Jewish Ghetto by the Germans in Warsaw; the poor unfortunates being herded together under the most dreadful living conditions, their persecutors claiming that this was a health measure.

Councillor J. Hoult, who was our Mayor that year, urged all Ilkestonians to 'Play your part in the building of a promising future.' And so through the National Savings, Red Cross Savings schemes and the Spitfire Fund, our townspeople really dug in their heels, and by 1941, a staggering £200,000 was raised by the end of War Weapons' Week.

Besides digging deep into their pockets, Ilkestonians, along with others throughout Britain, also began digging for Victory, planting every available bit of ground with vegetables, so that they were assured of food for the oncoming year.

We were lucky enough to rent an allotment in some gardens at the back of our Gas Works, about a quarter of an hour's walk away. It was too late to plant potatoes, but we did set cabbage plants, ready for the Spring, and we got stuck into the digging and raking, ready for our planting early the following year. And there was an old greenhouse, minus several panes, and so we started to mend that too.

I used to dig alongside John, and loved the feel and smell of the newly turned soil. When the dark evenings closed in on us, we planned what we'd grow next year, and I begged a part all to myself, 'Just for some flowers – to brighten things up a bit.'

And we sure needed brightening up, I can tell you. Not many nights passed but that we could hear distant sirens.

'Sounds as if they're getting it over Derby or Nottingham,' we'd say. Some people would go into the brick Air Raid shelters which stuck out like sore thumbs in all our streets. Others would occupy their own tin shelters, sunk below ground level in their back gardens.

Black out curtains would be drawn tight against panes already criss-crossed with wide strips of gummed paper, to cut down the risk of shattering glass, should a bomb or shrapnel drop nearby; and woe betide anybody who showed a chink of light. An Air Raid Warden would bang on the offending door, 'Put that ruddy light out,' he'd yell.

The odd car caught out at this time would have dipped, and shaded head-lights, and pedestrians would be shuffling along in the darkness with torch lights pointed at the ground.

Everywhere it was total black-out.

When the all-clear sounded its vibrant, triumphant sound we'd all send up a fervent prayer of thanks.

I think the people of Britain must have prayed more at that period than at any other time in their lives.

Chapter Three

The dark Winter of 1940, made even darker by the blackout restrictions, was upon us. Christmas was fast approaching, and we were determined to make it as bright and happy as was possible. Which meant improvising again. Christmas baubles, and tinsels, unless one had them left from previous years were definitely out – all raw materials being channelled into the war effort.

John cut me a large, twiggy branch off a tree, which I painted with white-wash, and hung with baubles made out of coloured wools, or covered with silver paper.

I knitted him a Balaclava helmet and some long socks, for he worked outside at Stanton. At this time nearly all women were knitting socks, and helmets, for the forces at home and over-seas.

Our Mam was in her element, knitting squares which she sewed up into blankets, for use by the Red Cross, and St John's Ambulance. She had already received one letter of thanks, from the Central Depot, for her first efforts.

One of John's mates gave him a rabbit he'd snared, in a field outside the Stanton works, so we were alright for a Christmas dinner, and our precious ration coupons made sure we had a plum pud and mince pies, and some tobacco for Our Dad's and the old man's pipes, and some chocolates for Our Mam.

And all the time news was coming over the wireless of the North African campaign, of Cunningham's ships bombarding the Italian positions and of General Wavell's attacks on other divisions.

Hitler was planning to invade Greece, and to crush Soviet Russia in a rapid campaign.

The 6th Australian Division, we were told, was moved into Africa, and a concentrated attack by tanks and artillery resulted in 30,000 Italian prisoners being taken.

And then the bombing of Malta by the Germans and Italians began. Each morning when we arrived at the factory we'd discuss the previous day's news.

'I'nt it awful? All them soldiers an' airmen gettin' killed. Some poor Mother's sons.'

'Aye', an' it's same on th'German's side. Bet their Mothers are grievin' as well. The've all bin' babies at some time, poor sods.'

The weather seemed to echo the news too. If it was a horrible wet day you could be sure the news on the wireless would be bad too.

Posters were plastered onto walls all over the town, in shops, offices, banks, and on factory walls, warning us that Careless Talk Costs Lives, and urging us to Dig For Victory.

Which was what we were all doing by the Spring of 1941. We set seeds and planted potatoes and cabbage plants. John and I had by this time mended the greenhouse, and got the old boiler system working. We were offered lots of coal slack off the neighbouring garden holders, many of whom were colliers; so we tried growing our own tomato plants from seed. I set trays of flower seeds too – determined to bring a bit of colour into our gloomy, war-time existence. We sure needed something to cheer us up.

It was heaven to be by ourselves down at the garden, working side by side, away from the stifling confines of the terraced house, noisy neighbours, and the constant vigilance of the old man, and the awareness that this shared existence would never be my true home.

There was a great campaign going too, at this time to Make Do And Mend. Old coats were cut up to make jackets and trousers and dresses for the children. I was in great demand, for I had learned dressmaking and alterations at an Evening Class.

So, I was able to earn an extra bob or two, which went into a 'kitty' for buying new furniture, for if ever we got our own home. That is if we weren't all blown to smithereens before that day dawned.

We were able to buy large panels too, of sub-standard parachute silk, all white, and which was excellent for making blouses, nighties and underwear. A few sprigs of flowers worked with coloured silks and we had undies to be proud of.

By this time I had managed to buy an old, treadle sewing machine for about thirty bob. How I polished that machine, and oiled it. I had waited for SO many years for a possession like this. Dad had been promising to buy me one for all of my young life; but somehow he never seemed to have the money; most of his spare cash going to The Trumpet, The Ancient Druids or The Derby Arms. Dear old Dad – he always meant well.

One evening a week I would go on all-night duty at the Chaucer Street A.R.P. Post, usually when I wouldn't be working at the factory next day. One of the well trained Red Cross workers, or St John's Ambulance people would give us further instruction in First Aid. Some of us would inevitably drop off to sleep, but always there were others on full alert.

The sirens would start to wail, turning our blood to water, filling our stout hearts with fear. What would this night bring forth?

We would all congregate on an inner corridor, this being voted the safest place in the school, away from windows and splintering glass.

How we'd sigh with relief when the All Clear sounded. Dear God – thank you, was the silent prayer we all sent heavenwards.

And then, one morning early in May, when I'd just come off night duty I was sick in the street, and I realised that I was pregnant.

The knowledge shattered me, for I had vowed I'd never bring a child into this War torn world.

By the time I arrived home John had already left for work, so I'd have to wait until that evening before I told him my news. How would he take it, I wondered? Would he be pleased?

That day seemed the longest of my life.

Chapter Four

'You'll be alright love,' was how my husband John greeted the news that I was expecting our first child. 'What has to be will be; an' you know I shall always take care of you.'

At the factory next morning I just couldn't keep the news to myself, and by half past eight the whole of the winding room knew too. Then, I realised that one of the women who lived near to my old home might JUST see Our Mam, and tell her. I didn't want that to happen, so instead of eating my sandwiches in the factory canteen I hurried the half mile there myself.

'What's up Else?' Mam wanted to know, so out it came.

'I'm going to have a baby Mam. It'll be about Christmas time.' Mam was that pleased, as most first Grandmas are.

'Yer'll hae' to pack up work, won't ya' – in a bit?' Then – 'I'll see if I've got some old sheets yer' can cut up – ready fer'd crib,' she told me.

Back at the factory I felt sick with all that rushing about, so Mrs Farnsworth, who mashed all our tea, made me a strong cup, and told me to sit down for a while.

'Looks to me as though yo' expectin',' she said.

'Yes – I am,' I felt lousy. Did it show that much, I wondered?

After that life went on pretty much as before. Air raids over the large cities, planes shot down over the Channel and the Continent.

The Germans began to attack the Island of Crete, and in the Atlantic their submarines were sinking our ships.

In North Africa Field Marshall Rommel was massing his troops off the Egyptian border. Good heavens, that's where

1 Desert Battle Scenes in Africa

my younger brother Harold, was stationed. He was with
Wavell's force. He had joined the Army when he was just
seventeen, and was one of the first to be drafted abroad.

I began to feel uneasy, which didn't help the sickness I
was having every morning.

In the Mediterranean the little island of Malta was
fighting for survival, with our convoys struggling to get
through with much needed supplies, and we were told of
the bravery of the crews of The Ark Royal, The Renown, of
Nelson and of the Aircraft Carrier Victorious, and we sent
up a fervent prayer of thanks each time we heard that
supplies had got through.

About this time the infamous Lord Haw-Haw, born in
Brooklyn, son of an English mother and Irish father, started
subjecting us to an amazing propaganda of fact and fiction
about the triumph of the Nazis, of devastation by their
bombers, and of ships being sunk.

'This is Jairmany calling,' was how he started his
broadcasts, trying to undermine the confidence and
morale of the British people.

'T'on that bugger off' was how he was usually greeted. 'Wae' dunna want ta' lissen' ta' 'im – aye' wants shootin' out'ud way,' a sentiment we all echoed.

Evacuees were still being moved into the safer, small towns and villages. I well remember a family called Henley, who had come from bomb scared London, and moved into a terraced house in the next street to us. They never went back again, and most of the family, auburn haired and freckled, are still here.

There was one thing which stood out above all else at that troubled time, and that was the comradeship everybody showed to each other, the helping hand freely offered, old feuds forgotten, neighbours' quarrels pushed into the background, for we were all united in our fear, fear that every day would be our last.

Then at Mam's one day the postman called with an official looking envelope. When Mam had read it she kept on saying, over and over again,

'Oh my God – oh my God.' It was short. 'Your son Harold . . . missing in Tobruk . . . believed to be captured by the German Army.'

I put my arms round Mam.

'But Mam, he'll be alive. He'll just be a prisoner of War.' I consoled her, and after a while she calmed down.

Poor Mam, and all those other Mums who were grieving for their sons.

The year wore on and I was getting bulky so decided to pack up work. I left with plenty of good advice ringing in my ears.

'Yer' want ta' get plenty o' raspberry leaf tea down yer'.'

Another told me to, 'Keep rubbing olive oil on yer' belly. It'll get rid 'od stretch marks.'

I was attending the Ante-Natal clinic regularly, and taking my quota of orange juice and cod liver oil, AND reading all the medical articles about pregnancy that I could lay my hands on. I still couldn't get any advice from our Mam about what to expect.

By this time I had finished at the A.R.P. Post, so had

plenty of time for knitting and sewing baby clothes. A neighbour sold me a good strong cot for a few bob, and by the end of November we had bought a new, smallish type pram. I was like a kid with a new toy, patting the silken pillow and rearranging the pram cover. John was getting as excited as I was.

But in spite of our anticipation we were still very much aware of what was happening in the War zones.

President Roosevelt was appealing to the Japanese Emperor for a peaceful settlement to the situation in the Pacific, but all in vain.

On the Seventh of December, American warships sheltering in Pearl Harbour were attacked by wave after wave of Japanese bombers. It was still early in the morning, and the crews of the ships were caught off guard. The devastation was terrible, Cruisers, Destroyers, as well as battleships being sunk, and many lives were lost.

And all this had happened before the Japs and Americans were officially at war. But on December Eighth, the United States and Britain finally declared war on Japan, after President Roosevelt had described the tragedy at Pearl Harbour as 'A date which will live in infamy.'

So – we were now at war with Japan as well as Germany.

What devious weapons would the Japs use against us, and our troops, we wondered.

The Old Man was still regaling us with stories about the Boer War, and of the natives who fought with assegais, and we would listen to him patiently.

But I was far more impatient about my big event, and by Christmas I was still waiting. Oh, but he was a lively baby; there was never any doubt in my mind but that it would be a boy. Every little movement and I'd be counting the minutes – could this be it?

Christmas came and went; New Year's Eve was celebrated quietly. Then on January 6th the time had come. Of course it had to be 2 o'clock in the morning, so, not wanting to bother anybody with a car at that time we walked the half mile or more, through the dark streets and

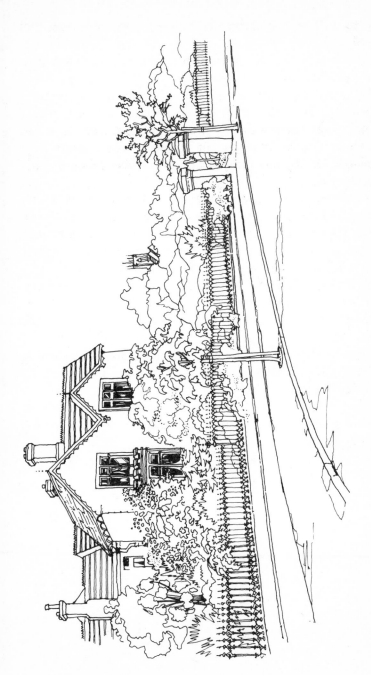

2 Ilkeston Maternity Home

up the hill to the Maternity Home – right opposite the Cemetery.

At the door the Night Nurse took the small case off John and said brusquely,

'You can go home; she'll be alright now. Ring in the morning.' Then she took me upstairs to a large, empty room, examined me briefly then said, 'Get undressed and into bed. You're not ready yet – try to get some sleep.'

Sleep? On the most important day of my life, next to my wedding day.

All through that long night I lay and listened to St Mary's Church clock chiming every quarter hour. 'Top Choch clock' we used to call it. The full moon lit up the room with its six or so empty beds, and I was alone with my anxiety and pain, several times on my knees beside the bed.

At 7 a.m. Night Nurse poked her head round the door, took one look at me, then,

'My God' she said, and shouted for help along the corridor.

Ten minutes later it was all over and I lay back, exhausted. But when Sister placed the tiny bundle in my arms and said,

'You have a lovely baby son my dear,' all my tiredness was forgotten, and I put out eager arms for my baby – my first born.

Chapter Five

The months which followed were some of the happiest of my life, for wasn't I now fulfilled as a Mother, my first born a son?

A Queen couldn't have been happier than I was at that time.

But there was one cloud in the sky, a huge, ominous black cloud. The War which seemed to be waging all over the Northern Hemisphere and which had now spread to the Phillipines, to Malaya and the East Indies, with our Forces retreating, and in North Africa, the German troops, led by Rommel, were still advancing.

The brave people of Malta were being bombarded night and day. How much longer, we wondered, before they were finally defeated?

We had named our son, John, after his father. Even before he was born it was 'our John this' and 'our John that'. When my husband went to register the birth the Registrar asked him,

'And what name has been chosen?'

'Er –' my husband thought for a while, then – 'We'd better call him John,' he told the astonished man.

'That's funny,' the Registrar said, 'Most Fathers tell me the name as soon as they come through that door.'

So John it was. At birth he had dark brown hair, but by the end of three weeks it had changed to a shiny cap of red; not auburn, but bright carrot red hair. That caused some comments, some ribald remarks, I can tell you.

'Has the milkman got red hair, or is it the postman?' I was repeatedly asked.

'Oh no – it's the butcher,' I would answer, playing along with them.

I had decided to feed the baby myself, that being the natural, the accepted thing to do at that time. There WERE some artificial baby foods on the market, but only a few. I found that breast feeding was the most satisfying experience, and often regret that today's Mothers, figure conscious Mums, either for reasons of vanity, or just that they think that breast feeding is somehow unpleasant, are missing out on the great joy that natural feeding can bring.

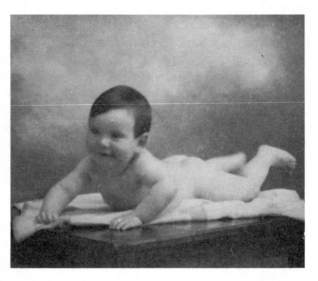

3 My Son John: at six months

My days were so full at that time, what with feeding, nappy changing (Terry towelling nappies, not throw away pads like today), washing, ironing, keeping the house clean, and cooking, I barely had time to take my baby out in his pram.

But when I did, oh my – I was as proud as the proverbial peacock. Not being used to pram pushing, at first I steered a somewhat erratic course. I felt so self-conscious at my first efforts. Then of course I was repeatedly stopped by friends and neighbours, who O-ohed and Ah-hd, and exclaimed at the baby's bright red hair.

When John and I took him out for walks at the weekend, I was almost bursting with happiness, and now, all these years later when I see a couple pushing their first-born in a new pram, I feel a great surge of pleasure for them, and a great longing inside me.

Each evening when John came home from work he would bend over his leg-kicking, chuckling young son and say,

'Hello my little pigeon – where ya' bin'? Hae' ya' bin' to peepies?' and young John would kick harder, wave his podgy arms and blow bubbles at his Dad. This would make the Old Man chuckle too, for he thought the world of this new grandson.

And so the long, hot Summer wore on, me enjoying my role as Mother, every morning awakening with a new zest for life, every day a fresh challenge.

Yet all the time we were sharply and painfully aware of the War – of the bombing over Britain, of the Burma Campaign, of the Battle of the Atlantic and the Mediterranean. Scarcely a day went by but that the Air Raid sirens sounded, and we would listen to the skies above us, for the drone of planes; for we had learned to distinguish between the sound of the German's and our own planes.

We would go about our everyday tasks, listening, fearful of what might happen, not wanting to hide in the dark, damp, smelly street shelters, for they were often used as urinals, and courting rendezvous.

And our sighs and prayers of relief when the All Clear went was like coming back from the dead; seeing the sunshine for the first time.

By this time we all carried Identity Cards; buff coloured, double cards with our names and addresses inside – in case we were blown to bits by a bomb, I suppose. And we carried our gas masks with us always, as did some people with their ration books.

There were long queues at the butchers and bakers, and

especially the sweet shops, for if a special line in sweets had arrived, the word went round like wild-fire.

'Eh up – thee's had some Radiance toffee cum' in at Mrs Shelto aye' ya' got ya' coupons ready?'

I would often do a swop with a woman next door, toffee coupons and meat coupons for some of her bread coupons. We now had four ration books in the house, and with John wanting bread, lots of bread for sandwiches for work, and with us not using all our meat coupons, well – it seemed the sensible thing to do.

There were plenty of shady, black market deals going on.

'Could ya' do wi' a bit of extra bacon. Ah' know this bloke as' as a pig he aint declared,' or 'Could your Master do wi' some trousers an' workin' boots? Ah' know where ya' can get some – now't said.'

We weren't too conscientious over these dealings, it was happening all over the place, and it gave a lift to our often sagging morale to get what we looked on as 'somatt for now't'. But we still had to pay for the blessed extras.

By August of 1942 we were told that the attacks on Malta were less severe, but that in New Guinea the Japs were making great advances, and pushing back the Australian Divisions. Many ships were being sunk in the Atlantic, with the U-boats harrassing the North Atlantic convoy routes.

Unbelievably the U.S. Secretary of State was urging the formation of an International Peace Keeping Organisation by the United Nations after the War. Talk about shutting the stable door after the horse had bolted.

In North Africa Rommel wasn't getting it all his own way. He had underestimated the British positions, and constantly had to withdraw. All this news which kept filtering through to us was greeted with elation.

But by the end of September I was not too elated with the news that my Doctor told me.

I had always been anaemic, especially since my adolescence, and did not pay too much attention to missed periods.

So – when I went to see my Doctor because I had been feeling a bit 'run down' and 'tissicky', I was amazed when he said,

'But my dear, didn't you know you were pregnant?' Pregnant? Again? But it was only eight months since I'd had my first baby.

I'm afraid that the War and everything connected with it faded from my mind with this latest shock. Whatever would people say?

Then – I shrugged my shoulders and accepted the news. Ah well – it wasn't the end of the world, was it?

Chapter Six

At the same time I learned I was expecting our second child, part of the War zone was extended to the Guadalcanal area, in the Solomons, with the Americans preparing to defend the island against the Japs.

Throughout November and December there was heavy fighting for supremacy, with the Americans constantly reinforcing their troops.

And now the Battle of Alamein was well under way, a careful and meticulous plan of campaign by Montgomery, and helped along by the Australian Divisions.

We would sit by our wireless sets in the evening, after I'd got the baby to sleep, listening, not speaking much – just weighing everything up. The old man would just sit there, stroking the stubble on his chin. John would be puffing at his pipe, with his newspaper half open on his knee, and I would be knitting or sewing. And when the news finished we would start to speculate.

'Is that good news d'you think?' I'd ask.

'Can't be bad if Montgomery's there,' John would answer. 'He's best leader we've got.'

'Thee want'a get round 'em wi' them assegais,' the old man would mutter, his mind still on the Boer War.

John was as taken aback about the news of a second baby as I had been. He was MOST concerned for me.

'We'll be alright love – we shall get through,' he consoled me. 'I hope I don't get called up though – not now,' he added as an afterthought.

At that time, in the early Forties, the Pill had not been

invented – birth control was very much a question of restraint – denial. There were certain methods, as used by the men; but lots of women relied on hot baths and liberal doses of gin; to put matters right as it were.

But if they were unlucky enough to 'get in the family way', a term very much in evidence at that time, well – it was just too bad; they had to make the best of it.

Large families were still very much in fashion, but now, not quite as much as in the early nineties.

Christmas was a quiet affair for us that year. It was evident that I wasn't going to be too well over this baby. Morning sickness seemed to last most of the day. I felt TERRIBLE. The New Year came and went, again quietly for us.

The Russians began an offensive around Stalingrad, and soon the Germans had to retreat. Churchill and Roosevelt met in Casablanca to discuss the Japanese's situation. It was suggested that the British could be more on the offensive with the Japanese. Mercifully a split between us and the Americans was averted.

And then the Old Man became ill. Most Winters he'd get a bad attack of bronchitis, but this year it was worse. He took to his bed, upstairs, and I had the unenviable task of fetching and carrying; washing the old fella and feeding him; emptying his po, a feeling of nausea sickening me each time I did so. I was told by a neighbour that I could borrow a bed-pan from the Holy Trinity Church – which I did so. It was much less strain for me than to have to help him out of bed on to the po, as I had been doing.

As I got heavier and bulkier the stairs appeared to get steeper, so that by the end of the day I was absolutely exhausted. The Old Man started to be incontinent, and as he liked to wear his long pants in bed, as well as his singlet – you can imagine the amount of washing it made every day.

Finally, in desperation I asked John to get his bed downstairs, where I could take care of him better.

Although there was a large family of brothers and sisters

I was in sole charge of the Old Man's nursing, and comfort. But he was so grateful, and he'd often say,

'Thow't a good lass. Our Johnnie's a lucky fella'.'

And the war still raged on.

Throughout the Spring we heard of the fighting in Tunisia, and the Eastern Front, in Burma and the Solomons; and in May, of another Dambusters pass over Germany.

By the end of the month I knew I wouldn't have too long to wait before my second baby was born. I was to have the confinement at home, with a Midwife attending, a Nurse Bannister.

'We shall have to get your bed back upstairs,' John told his Dad. 'Elsie'll have to be downstairs in the front room.' So, with a lot of grumbling the old fella slept upstairs again. A spare single bed was brought down for me, and I began the long waiting game.

Fortunately, young John was a good baby, slept well and didn't cry a lot; but he was still not quite a year and a half, and still needed a lot of attention.

As well as looking after the old man and the baby I still did all my own washing and cleaning, and cooking, AND all the shopping so it was no wonder that I felt exhausted by the evening.

The Air-Raid sirens wailed their warning almost every night, and as there was an Anti-aircraft gun now at the back of Heanor Road we would hear the sharp, shrill sound of firing from that, and the ping of bits of shrapnel falling onto the streets.

On June 7th I started to feel the first labour pains; slow, heavy, agonising. The Midwife was sent for.

'Not yet', she told me. 'You could go another day.'

Two days later she called Dr Myers.

'I'm not too happy about this one,' she told him. He examined me. 'We'll have to get the water going,' he poked the huge lump. 'About time you got rid of this, young lady. Just a little snip.' He snipped, and the Midwife jumped back.

'I've got a ruddy shoe full,' she told the laughing Dr Myers, who announced he'd be back later.

He was – right in the middle of an Air-raid alert. I was too far gone to care whether bombs started dropping or not. I hoped my baby was going to be alright; I'd now been in labour for about three days.

The Doctor announced that he was going to hurry things up. He produced forceps and a pad on which he poured something out of a bottle, and put under my nose.

'Now then me' girl, I want you to start counting.' I did. 'One– two — three —— four —— five — bangbang — guns —— se–vern—' A sharp pain and I was away.

My face was being slapped, gently, and a female voice urged me to 'Come on Mother – wake up.' A baby was squalling, a long way off.

Slowly I surfaced, and a warm bundle was placed in my arms, and the same voice said,

'See here, Mother – you've got a lovely baby boy.'

'But I've already got a boy; we wanted a girl.' Then I looked down at the pink, screwed up face. 'But his head's all twisted.'

The poor mite, I thought, looked grotesque, and the skin on one ear had been torn.

'Oh, that's only the forceps,' Nurse Bannister told me. 'He'll be alright in a few days. He's a lo-ovely baby.'

But I thought he looked more like a frog, and said so. The Doctor told me he was lucky to be alive.

'He's a healthy baby; and he's got all the bits and pieces in the right places.'

And after I'd suckled him and he was asleep I felt the same fierce pride that I'd felt over my first born.

The Ack Ack was still booming away, and enemy planes still droned high above us.

'Please God – don't let us die; not now; not like this.'

I prayed, as I snuggled my new baby up to me, and held on to young John, who was peeping over the side of the bed. My husband looked on anxiously, then went into the kitchen to make me a life-saving cup of tea.

Chapter Seven

1943 was a year I'd not ever want to live through again. Here was I with a new baby, and my first one only fifteen months old; a badly old man to care for, and a hard working, hungry husband to cook for each evening. Rationing was in full swing and so was the abominable war, with the air raid sirens going almost every night.

With all the extra work a new baby entailed, and with the Old Man still being incontinent on occasions, well – you can imagine the amount of washing I had every day. I was tired all the time so it was no wonder my milk gradually dwindled, and the baby, Ron, cried continuously. He'd keep us awake half the night, and the neighbours began to complain.

'I'll have to put him on artificial milk,' I told my husband.

'Good – then perhaps we can all get some sleep.'

So I put him on National Dried Milk and the change was miraculous. He was soon putting on weight.

Mam used to call sometimes to take him out in his pram, to give me a break. She lived a mile and a half away from us. She was most concerned about me.

'Ya' want to tek' care o' yer'sen. Ya' don't want ta' ay' any more kids just yet.' But still she didn't tell me how to avoid 'getting into the family way' again. How things have changed!!

Mam had her own cross to bear at this time. Harold was still a prisoner of war, and that, of course was a great worry to her. Dan was now married and lived in his own semi-detached house at the other end of town; but Marie, the youngest, had grown into a shy, withdrawn girl and

4 My mam with John and young Ron

would not play with other children, either in the payground or at home. She was such a pretty girl, with soft, pink skin, grey eyes and shiny dark brown hair. Much prettier than I was and of course, being the baby of the family, well – we all idolised her.

But one day the Headmistress sent for our Mam.

'Did you know your daughter is backward,' she told her. 'She will NOT mix with the other children. Just sits in the cloakroom all playtime; it's not natural.' Mam was most indignant. She didn't want anybody else confirming what she already suspected.

There were no special schools around us at that time, for mentally subnormal children, no Rehabilitation Centres as there are now – no Stanton Vales schools.

And so the poor, unfortunate girl withdrew more and more into her own little silent world.

Mam kept all these worries hidden, never unburdening herself to others. She was a real 'tough 'un' was Our Mam. Dad just shook his head sadly if I tried to talk to him about it. Poor Dad. Poor Mam . . . Poor Marie.

And so 1943 wove its unsteady, uneasy way towards another Christmas; uneasy because the threat of air raids was still very much with us.

Christmas was a utility time again that year, with homemade presents being in the premium. I well remember a cake recipe I used at that time, with all sorts of available fruit, dates, apples, prunes; and the marzipan a mixture of Soya bean flour, strongly flavoured with almond essence, and the thinnest coating of icing sugar. But with a fancy paper frill it looked like the real thing.

All the ingredients for cake making were in very short supply; even the hens seemed to have stopped laying, and we had to use a bright yellow substance called Egg Powder. But with a bit of ingenuity you could do lots of things with it. One of our favourites was egg fritters. The powder was mixed with self-raising flour and a little milk, and spoonsful were dropped into hot fat for a minute. Delicious – and even more delicious with a little grated onion and cheese thrown in. I had managed to save a tin of pink salmon; the red variety being almost unobtainable, and I secretly coloured it with a few drops of cochineal. No one seemed to notice the difference – anyway, the salmon flavour was there.

I had knitted sweaters and socks and gloves for the men folk, and John had made a pull-along cart for young Johnnie, brightly painted with red, and that little homemade toy was taken everywhere with him. I often wonder why some parents think they have to spend so much money on toys, sometimes several hundreds of pounds. Just look at today's computerised toys. It's a well known fact that the youngsters often prefer the box in which the thing came in to the toy itself.

5 Toys . . . a home-made menagerie

For the baby I made several soft toys out of scraps of material. I had a paper pattern which covered all sorts of toy animals. I well remember one day showing a neighbour a rabbit and an elephant I'd made. She asked me if I'd make one for her youngster, paying me of course. Inevitably another neighbour came along, as did several others, and I was soon turning out a Noah's Ark of stuffed toys.

The sideboard top was filled with bodies, and it reminded one of the Nutcracker Suite. I full expected them to come to life. There were ducks and elephants, rabbits and teddy bears, and dolls with pink velvet faces, their long plaits made out of yellow wool, and with eyes and mouths embroidered on, giving full rein to my artistic talents. The teddy bears had move-about arms and legs, these being wired through the body, a very tricky operation.

I was writing to a nephew, Jimmy Burns, at the time. He was with the Artillary Forces in Northern India, and I told him about my thriving, homemade toy business. By return of post he sent me requests from two of his mates, and accompanied by two pound notes for teddy bears to be despatched to two addresses in England. And I was thrilled when I got letters from the Mums thanking me for the 'wonderful teddies'.

An elderly bachelor named Tom, who was a friend of ours, gave me a large bundle of clothes which had belonged to his mother. There was a velvet cape, two fur fabric coats and several pieces of silk. It was a treasure trove, and you should have seen his eyes light up when I showed him the resulting toys I'd made.

In the two months preceding Christmas I had earned £20 with my toy sales. Now £20 at that time was a lot of money, so I put it in the Post Office Bank, and hoped that we'd be able to use it towards the sea-side holiday we'd planned when the war ended.

Another innovation during those war years was the use we made of blankets; the coarse, grey and brown variety. We'd fashion them into siren suits for the children, coats for ourselves with baggy, raglan sleeves, and also dressing gowns. Trimmed around the edges with blanket stitch using brightly coloured wools and we had warm, servicable clothes.

There was heartening news at this time of the proposed

campaign by the British and American Forces; General Eisenhower to be the Supreme Allied Commander for the Invasion of Europe, with General Montgomery leading the British Forces; Air Marshall Mallory and Admiral Ramsay to lead the Air and Naval Forces. The Soviets were pushing back the Fourth Panzer Army and penetrating deeper and deeper into their territory. OH – it was such good news and gave a much needed boost to our flagging morale.

I hoped I wouldn't get pregnant again whilst the war was on. It was no time to be bringing children into the world. And so the New Year dawned; 1944, and with the advancement of all our Allied Forces in the various War Zones, and news that our heavy bombers were attacking Berlin, a fervent prayer went heavenwards that this year would be the beginning of the end of our nightmare four years.

'Dear God – let it soon be over,' we'd pray every night.

Chapter Eight

I was so busy the following year, 1944, that I'm afraid the war was very much in the background as far as I was concerned. Young Johnnie was now two years old, a quiet, well behaved little boy. The Old Man followed him everywhere; when he played on the street with his little truck, and when he went to the lav at the bottom of the back yard. He just simply idolised him.

The baby Ron was getting big and bonny, with a head covered with golden curls. Everybody stopped to admire

6 Grandad Gadsby with 2 year old John

him. For the first few weeks of his life he scarcely uttered a murmur.

'What a good baby he's going to be,' I told my husband. But GOSH! when he did start to cry – bawl I should say, there was no stopping him. He wasn't so bad during the daytime, but night-time was proving to be a battle of wills.

Ron'd start up about midnight, howling as hard as he could, trying to waken the whole street. I'd leave him as long as I could bear, then I'd have to check to see if he was wet, or hungry, or full of wind.

'Can't you shut him up,' John would grumble. 'I've got to go to work tomorrow.' And of course, that made me resentful. I, too, had my full share of work next day. I, too, was losing sleep.

Some days I was so tired I scarcely knew what I was doing, and my cooking and washing and cleaning was done in an automatic daze. Often I'd be jolted into wakefulness with the Old Man calling,

'Yer'd better come an' see ta' young Johnnie. Looks like ay's put summat in 'is breeches agen'.' And there I'd find the lad, crouched down over a plaything, his rear view looking like the backside of a duck, an ominous lump weighing down his pants. I'd sigh. 'All in a day's work' I'd tell myself, as I went back to my yelling baby.

The war news was still coming to us over our wireless sets, of attacks and counter attacks by all sides; in the Pacific, on the Western Front, and of the advancement of the Russian Fourteenth Army towards the Danube. We'd hear of how many ships were being sunk, of plane losses on both sides, of casualties both in the Forces and civilians killed in air raids. We'd hear of our own townspeople receiving the dreaded telegram 'Regret – your son killed on active service.'

A few days after the baby Ron's first birthday, the first V1 Flying Bomb landed in England and killed six civilians. What other fiendish weapons had Hitler in store for us, we wondered? But at the same time we heard that two

Japanese Commanders had committed suicide – Hari-Kari, rather than give in to the advancing Americans.

And at the Nazi headquarters in East Prussia, an attempt was made by the Resistance to blow up Hitler. The Senior Officers and Politicians were at last trying to bring to an end, this mad-man's reign of terror.

By the end of August, Paris had been freed, and Marseilles and Toulon; and German Generals were surrendering.

And then the terrible concentration camps were being discovered. In the Majdanek camp alone thousands of people had been murdered by the Germans. Horrific!!

And so the year wore on, and somehow we managed with our rations and a lot of ingenuity. Once again I made a selection of soft toys for Christmas – a bit more money put towards our promised holiday.

Siren suits, the all in one, cosy, step-in hooded garments were very much the fashion for youngsters, and I made one each for my two boys; dark green boucle cloth, lined with plaid and bought with clothing coupons. Wooden clogs were very much the 'in' thing too, so I bought those to complete the outfits.

Ron had grown so fast he was now as big as young Johnnie, and the boys were taken for twins, and looked like a couple of gnomes walking beside me. Oh – I was so proud now that I had my two sons, and they looked so healthy with their fresh, pink complexions, John with his red hair and Ron with an abundance of golden curls. When the weather was sunny I'd take the children up to the Rec, a lovely open space on the west side of Ilkeston, and with breathtaking views over the fields, and up towards Shipley and West Hallam.

I'd pack a flask and sandwiches, and we'd stay there for hours, playing ball games; and the War seemed a million miles away. To one side and below the Rec was the Golf Links, that playground of the wealthy; and at this particular time a farmer was allowed to graze his sheep there. And THAT meant sheep-droppings.

'Just right for'd muck tub outside th' greenhouse,' John told me.

The greenhouse was a big, old 22 ft structure left by the former tenant of the allotment garden. So – this gal', ever resourceful, would take a small sack on these picnic jaunts, and we'd collect droppings on our way home. They were usually hard and dry, so easy to gather.

'Currants Mammy' young Johnnie said as he picked his first handful.

'DON'T – put them in your mouth.' I told him. 'It's po-oh po-oh'.

The baby would be crawling about on all fours, trying to help. Towards teatime we'd trundle back home, the sack perched precariously on the front of the pram, and Johnnie trotting on tired little legs beside us. And as we turned into our cul-de-sac street of drab, terraced houses, and with two ugly, brick air-raid shelters making it look even more hideous, my heart would sink to my tired feet, and I'd vow, over and over again that someday I'd break away from this prison; away to where the air was fresh and pure, and the surroundings more attractive. I was beginning to hate this environment, and could feel my nerve getting edgy, beginning to feel a neurotic tendency which was to manifest itself in later years.

But this was 1945, the beginning of the end as far as the War was concerned. The British and American Forces were advancing rapidly on the Western Front, but revealing as they did so, more Concentration Camps, and the horror of these hundreds of dead and dying victims. The notorious Belsen and Buchenwald camps were liberated, and here in our safe little homes were sickened and disgusted, as the full significance of these torturous crimes by the madman Hitler was revealed to us.

I'm afraid that people's beliefs in Christ and Christianity were greatly put to the test. As Our Mam and Dad said at that time,

'If there's a God in heaven why does he let such things happen.'

How often has that sentiment been echoed. But how often too, have the true believers prayed at these horrendous times,

'Forgive them Father, for they know not what they do.'

This was April, 1945. Surely from now on things could only get better. We could still hope and pray – still put our trust in this God we often doubted, so VERY often doubted.

Chapter Nine

Hitler is dead. So announced the World's radio at the beginning of May; immediately followed by the news that Goebbels and his wife had killed themselves and their six children. How tragic that the children had to suffer. They had been poisoned. But how the people rejoiced – the liberated millions on the Continent, the people back home.

Then, on May 7th, it was announced that the German forces had finally surrendered, and the following day was VE day, Victory in Europe, a victory against tyranny and oppression. King George VI and Winston Churchill made special broadcasts; there were bands parading the streets, special Thanksgiving Services in our churches, shop fronts were decorated with bunting and flags. The pubs did a roaring trade, and everywhere there were people milling around, laughing, shouting and singing, and generally letting their hair down.

Street parties were hastily arranged, tables laid together, sometimes the whole length of a street, with garlands and flags stretching above from window to window. The broad sticky tape, protection against flying glass was joyfully peeled off windows and pictures of the King and Queen put there instead.

A neighbour, Vera Dawson and I arranged our street party, begging funds from all the shopkeepers in the area, who gave willingly. Neighbours promised sandwiches, cakes, trifles, and we used the money collected to buy lemonade and prizes for the children, for we had planned fancy dress competitions and other games. The men in the street knocked together a stage for impromptu singing,

7 VE Day Street Party

and comic turns. Oh – it was chaotic the amount of planning we'd put in, and everybody seemed to be getting in each other's way. But everywhere was good humour and laughter.

8 Myself and John outside 14 Slade Street
during VE celebrations

Fancy dress was hurriedly made from scrap materials, and Mrs Shelton completely ran out of crepe paper. The food was prepared and put on the tables half an hour before the party began, with reliable neighbours keeping away the marauding dogs, which seemed to appear out of thin air.

What a party we had, and how we all made up for lost time just gorging ourselves with all the goodies.

Then the singing and dancing began. Old Mr Wilson played his fiddle; there were mouth organs and a concertina, and John beat time with his bones – two in each hand; we called them 'nick-nacks', and everywhere there was laughter and singing and happy faces. 'Come on Elsegie' us a song,' someone called. So – greatly daring, I climbed on to the stage and sang, 'Daddy Wouldn't Buy Me a Bow-Bow.' And greatly encouraged by the ovation I got, I sang 'I Wouldn't Leave My Little Wooden Hut For You,' and wiggled my arms and hips like a Hula Hula dancer. Oh, how we celebrated, for wasn't the nightmare now over? Or part of it, for the Japs were still fighting hard in the Philippines and Borneo.

But Trueman and Churchill had an ace they were about to play, and warned the Japs that they would not hesitate to use THE BOMB. Then on August 6th, 1945, the first Atom bomb, equal to 20,000 tons of T.N.T. was dropped on Hiroshima. 80,000 people were killed, and the city almost totally destroyed. Then – two days later, another Atom bomb was released, this time on Nagasaki, when another 40,000 were killed. Again, total devastation. This was too much for any nation to endure, and the Japanese Emperor, Hiroshita admitted defeat, and by August 15th, VJ day, it was all over, and an excuse for further rejoicing; more bands, more church services, more street parties, and more singing.

Each and every one of us felt liberated. Women started to wear trousers, a practical garment with Land Army workers which had now spread to everyday life. I had bought a pattern, and made a pair; grey with a white stripe; and on the final day of rejoicing when everybody was streaming toward the Market Place for a massive Service of Thanksgiving I donned my new trousers. They didn't exactly match my tweed, checked jacket, and I got some curious looks as we walked up the hill, our two sons clutching our hands, and wondering what all the fuss was about. But – I was making a gesture towards Women's Lib, and I felt defiant and elated.

S'funny, isn't it, how things like this stick in your mind. After all these days of rejoicing the Prisoners of War started to come home, and there was more celebrating in the town. Mam was told the date of Harold's return, and we planned a welcoming party, and hung a huge banner (one of Mam's old sheets) out of the bedroom window, with the words Welcome Home Harold printed in bright paint. There were banners like this all over the town, and every building and Church which had a flag pole, unleashed a whole array of Union Jacks, and more flags were stuck out of bedroom windows.

Never had the nation shown such rejoicing, never had the beer flowed so freely, and never had there been such a relaxing of morals, kissing and hugging going on with such a gay abandon.

'Thee's gun' to be a lot o' kids born after this lot,' our Mam told us. 'Yo' jus' mark my we'rds.' She was right of course, she always was.

But wasn't that the natural outcome of all periods of rejoicing?

Harold came home and had lots of stories to tell us, and Mam began to lose her strained look. But Harold never settled down to Army life after that, and soon got a job in Civvy Street. Then he began dating the girls.

Things began to quieten down after the rejoicing, and life gradually went back to normal. There was plenty of work for everybody, and lots of married women now stayed on at the factories and shops. Our Advertiser was full of vacancies for needle-workers, and offered good wages.

This was going to be the start of a New Era, with women often working for just 'pin-money', but mostly for better things for the home; new furniture, maybe a family car, new radios, and even the refrigerators the more wealthy people were buying. John had been going on for ages about a three-piece suite for the parlour, for up till now we'd never been able to afford one; so when he was offered a waiting-on job at the Live And Let Live he eagerly accepted it. It was a weekend job and made him a couple of pounds or more.

He handed the money over to me, and after a few weeks we were able to put a deposit on the suite: a brown, vinyl type. We now had some furniture in the parlour, and would sit in there at the weekends. The Old Man stayed put in his kitchen, so at last we had some time to ourselves.

Rationing lasted for a long time after this; the nation had to build up its sadly depleted reserves, and it was 1949 before clothes rationing ended.

And then, in the New Year, the Old Man took ill with bronchitis and pneumonia and was in bed for two weeks. He died about the middle of January.

This left a big gap in young Johnnie's life, for he idolised his Grandad. But it also meant that we were at last on our own. We could now begin to live a normal married life.

The War which had lasted for four weary years was over; rationing was gradually faded out, and we could at last abandon the horrible smelly gas-masks.

Our cities could start rebuilding; a mammoth task to be sure. But Oh – how many families were mourning loved ones, lost in the holocaust: fathers and sons lost in battle, women and children blown to bits by bombs. How much of our heritage had been destroyed: churches, historic buildings, fine houses?

But buildings could rise again, and, with time, hearts would gradually heal; but always the memory would be there. The whole nation would fervently vow, as people always do after these tragic times – 'We will NOT let it happen again. This is the War to end Wars.'

But – if I remember rightly – wasn't that what they said after the Great War in 1914?

Chapter Ten

Remembrance Day, November 11th, 1945 bore a double significance that year, for now we were paying homage to the thousands of valiant men who had been lost in the execution of their duty in two World Wars – fighting for Britain, for the right to be free.

Our cities and towns, and the coastal areas which had borne the full brunt of the bombing had started to rebuild. More goods were in the shops, people started to plan for holidays. We couldn't afford a holiday that year; all our spare cash was channelled into paying for the three-piece suite.

I started to look around at empty houses, houses for sale, a few to let. I walked for miles around the town; planning, hoping, searching. For I had grown to hate the small, dark, terraced house in this dead-end, back street where we lived.

I'd tell John when he came home, about the empty houses I'd seen.

'What – that old place?' he'd say. 'We're NOT buying that. Beside where's the money coming from? And what about having to leave our big garden?'

And so we stayed put, and I seethed and endured; but always the determination was there, to find a better place.

I spent more and more time down at the garden, and on Saturday mornings, would trundle the wooden barrow, a large box on two pram wheels, containing two delighted small boys, down past the gas-works. And I'd gather cabbages and brussel sprouts, rhubarb and asters and other flowers in season, and we'd push the barrow back home, young Ron usually finishing up on top, for he was a lazy child.

And when I got home, I'd bunch up the flowers, weigh the greens and pop around the neighbouring houses to see who wanted to buy. The home-grown tomatoes were always good sellers and over the years we'd built up a good clientele. All the proceeds went into the 'garden box', to buy seeds for the following season, and for a couple of loads of muck. Any money left over went into our 'holiday box.'

I was in charge of all the saving and expenditure; an unenviable chore I was lumbered with for the rest of our married life, sometimes building up a whole lot of resentment. But it was accepted that I was the better manager of the two; at least where money was concerned.

And so we saved and planned, and I decided, with John's approval of course, that when both boys were at Infant School, I'd look around for a part-time job. Then we'd save until we had enough for a deposit on a house.

Unhappily, things never happen according to plan, do they? But, I'll tell you about that later.

First – we were going to have a seaside holiday. My Aunt Ethel and Uncle Will at Nottingham, had a seaside bungalow at Ingoldmells, on The Haven site. It was a wooden, two roomed structure, painted black and white, and it had a verandah, with rambling roses struggling for survival in the salty air. So – we approached Aunt and Uncle and they said 'Yes – 'course you can have it for a week.'

Now at that time – early 1946, The Haven site was just a narrow field running from Ingoldmells Point Road, up to the grassy bank at the top, and directly down to the sea and sands. There were a few, corrugated iron, circular huts, and a straggle of other buildings, Nissen type huts. The lavatories were narrow, wooden privies, reached by a precarious climb up and over a wet, slippery bank. Water was obtained from a pump outside The Haven; the proprietor's house. But that was all part of the novelty of this outdoor life.

So – we planned the holiday for June. Young Johnnie was then four and a half and Ron, three years old. I bought an old cabin trunk, in which I packed all our bed linen, towels and clothes, and a van called on the Friday evening to collect. This chappie did a good trade for holiday makers for the East Coast, and his charges were very reasonable.

What excitement there was as the holiday drew nearer. I had knitted two swimsuit and cardigan sets for the boys, one in green and one in blue, and I'd also made a bathing costume for myself in a floral material, and I'd shirred it, so that it clung to my figure.

And so, early on the Saturday morning we walked the mile to the Great Northern Station, on Heanor Road. I was so excited when the steam train hissed its way towards the platform I thought I was going to have diarrhoea.

Oh but it was a lovely journey, and as we approached Boston, John declared he could smell the sea.

'Where Dad – where?' the boys wanted to know, and we exchanged knowing looks with each other. We were so happy to be taking our sons at last on our much awaited holiday.

Then we were at Skeggie, and waiting on Roman Bank for the bus that would take us the three miles to Ingoldmells. And when we reached the bungalow there was so much exploring to do: how to work the Primus stove, where to store the food away from the flies – no fridges remember. And of course the boys wanted to have their first view of the sea.

'Oh – isn't it big, Mammy?' a sentiment I had echoed all those years ago, when Aunt Ethel had taken me on my first memorable seaside holiday.

We were lucky. The weather was fine and warm all week, and every bit of our spare time was spent on the beach, building sand castles, collecting shells and playing ball games. Young Ron was content to play in the small puddles left by the tide, but Johnnie wanted to explore the white capped waves.

'I'm going for a dip,' I announced. I wanted to show off my new bathing costume, AND my slim figure. But you should have heard Ron – he screamed 'blue murder'; thought his Mam was going to disappear into the sea.

9 On holiday in Skegness

So – whilst John kept them occupied with buckets and spades I walked a considerable distance, until I could bathe in peace. Now, as I said, I was slim. Skinny would have been a better description. So – I'd put two pads of cotton wool inside the bathing costume, where my bust should have been.

It was alright whilst I splashed about in the water, but when I stood up; GOSH – the cotton wool felt like two wet jelly fish against my chest. So – turning away from some nearby bathers I squeezed, hard. Talk about the Fountains of Rome. Then I had to manipulate the wet lumps to their former position.

10 Husband John (extreme left) at Stanton

As I walked back towards my family, occasionally flopping down into the breakers I could feel the lumps sliding down again towards my tummy, and as I sprinted across the sand and a voice called out, 'I think you've dropped something Missus,' I pretended not to hear, and ran the rest of the way with my hands in a 'cross your heart' position.

That was the last time I tried to improve my figure with artificial means, and when a work-pal of my husbands, who was holidaying in the same place said to him,

'I wish my wife had a figure like your Missus,' well – I felt a whole lot better.

In the evening we'd walk down Sea Lane towards Ingoldmells Village. And we didn't have to dodge traffic, because there wasn't any.

Billy Butlins Camp wasn't the huge affair it is now, and most of their entertainment was inside the barbed wire enclosure. When we reached the Village we'd make for The Three Tuns and buy lemonade for the boys and glasses of beer for ourselves. There was one other pub in the Village and, as far as I can remember, a little general store, and a small, wet fish shop.

Ingoldmells at that time was a typical country village, with its square towered church sheltering a cluster of cottages. But when I visited it once, after an absence of ten years or more I couldn't believe my eyes. A Holiday Camp around every bend, with row after regimented row of caravans, and hideous concrete toilet blocks at either end. There must have been thousands of caravans, and the smell of chips and hot-dogs everywhere, and the monotonous sound of the Bingo caller.

They call this progress, don't they? But I call it total devastation; or perhaps desecration would be a better word.

But nothing would ever spoil the memory of our first seaside holiday as a complete family.

Chapter Eleven

The following two years were busy, happy ones. Each morning I'd wake with a new zest for life, every day was a challenge. I'd got a good, hard working husband and two healthy, young sons, and although I'd have liked a better place in which to live, I made the most of the house we'd got with fresh paint, attractive wallpaper and pretty curtains.

The War was over, Hitler was no more, long live our King and Queen.

Ilkeston was soon back to normal, fresh businesses starting, new shops opening up, plenty of jobs for everybody.

Aprt from a few bomb blasted areas, there was little to remind us of that devastating war. Of course, our lovely Victorian Park was now without its iron railings, as were many of our garden fronts. All these had been acquisitioned to help with munitions; and the parks and houses are still without their railings after more than forty years.

In the New Year I took young John along to the Infant's School at Holy Trinity, and he wasn't a bit of trouble; took to it like a little soldier. Of course, Ron missed his brother terribly and kept on saying:

'When can I start school?' He so much wanted to be like his brother; even wanted his curls cut off and his hair plastered down straight. 'So's it's like our John's.' Young John's was a lovely auburn shade, but straight as 'pump water'.

Of course it was all rush, getting to school for nine o'clock, back home to clean and cook and wash, then back to school to fetch Johnny for his dinner, then at school again for a quarter past one. And as school finished at 3.30, the afternoons just flew by.

By this time John had left his job as spare crane driver at Stanton, and gone to work at the Shipley Colliery. He was a wagon shunter on the coal trains, and hadn't been there long when he was offered the job as Traffic Foreman, controlling all the traffic between the Coppice and Shipley Pits. Sadly, the pits are no more, only a boiler house and head-stocks left to remind us of a once thriving heritage.

When it was Summer and holiday times I'd take the boys up to the lovely reservoir – trees along the west side with a steep, grassy hill leading up to Shipley Hall, and with rhododendrons clustering the opposite shore.

11 Shipley Hall

I'd sit there sketching, and the boys would be looking out for the coal trains which ran parallel with the Reservoir, and often their Dad would be riding up there in front.

One of the drivers loved to sing, and he'd be belting out hymns at the top of his voice, the sound carrying above the rattle and hiss of the steam driven engine.

We'd picnic beside the beautiful stretch of water, and I'd point out the various birds and wild-life there. I've never lost this love of Nature, and can sit for hours beside a lake, just watching the sunlight make millions of diamonds on the water, and I never cease to marvel at the antics of ducks, and geese and swans. Sometimes we'd spend whole days on the Rutland Rec, picnicing, playing ball games, or we'd just sit there soaking up the sun; anything to keep me away from the suffocating confines of the back street, with its noise and smells.

Then it was time for Ron to go to the Infant's School. He was alright till we got there, but when I started to come away, GOSH – all Heaven was let loose. He screamed; he fought; and it took the Headmistress and two teachers to restrain him.

'Quick Mother – off with you; he'll be alright,' the Headmistress told me, so, feeling a choking sensation I obeyed.

But when I went back to the school at dinner time, full of trepidation I was amazed to find him enthusiastic about his teacher, the other kids and what he'd been doing that morning; and, after dinner he couldn't wait to get back again. Another hurdle overcome.

So – now that both boys were at school I could at last think about a part-time job. There were plenty of jobs going, but I wanted one to fit in with school hours. I soon found one in a factory, but they wanted me to work until five o'clock. What to do about the boys though, after school. So I asked Our Mam if they could go there until John came from work. At first Mam said 'yes' so I arranged to start the job the following Monday. But by the weekend Mam had changed her mind, said it would be too much for her; but secretly, I don't think she approved of me going out to work, with two small children to care for.

So I looked round again, and this time was fortunate. I was offered a cutter's job at Lewis's Meridian factory at Ilkeston Junction. I was to work from ten until three in the afternoon. What luck. So – I learned to be a cutter in Room

23; cutting out men's underwear from an interlock fabric.

First I had to make a 'lay', with thick, cardboard patterns and using a black marker being very careful not to move the pattern. The 'lay' was then put to one side whilst I rolled out layer after layer of material from a huge roll on a pole at one end of the long table. Then, the 'lay' was carefully placed on top, and I had to start cutting round the marked pattern. And we used long cutting shears, almost as big as hedge clippers.

Just imagine cutting through a dozen layers of thick, interlock material with bare hands. In no time at all I had blisters on my thumb and forefinger, and had to go to the first-aid room. But after a while these blisters hardened off into lumps, 'cutter's lumps', and I have them to this day. I enjoyed the job; it was different from silk winding – I was learning a new trade; and anyway I was now earning, and able to save my whole wage every week.

John often used to bring the children to meet me, for his shift finished at three, and he was able to collect the boys from school. He put the saucepans containing vegetables, which I'd prepared that morning, on the hob beside the coal fire, so that we'd not have to wait long for our hot meal. Of course my spare time was taken up with household chores, but, although I was so thin I was strong and healthy, and took things in my stride.

Oh – everything was working out perfectly; our bank balance would soon grow; soon we'd have enough to put down on a house. A house of our own. How we planned and schemed for that dream house. We'd have a bathroom at last, instead of that tin bath beside the fire; and I'd have a proper, separate kitchen as well as a living room, and a front sitting room, with, maybe in time, one of those televisions which were becoming popular.

And of course, we'd have a large garden at the back with another greenhouse and a lawn, and flowerbeds, and a play area for the children. We'd choose a house in a nice part of town. Maybe Shipley, where there would be fields around us. We'd be SO happy – there was never any doubt about that.

Alas – 'the best laid plans of mice and men' and all that. I'd been at my new job, and getting really proficient for just five weeks when the blow fell. I was pregnant again. We COULDN'T believe it; we just COULDN'T take it in, but there it was. I'd have to pack up work. But first I was going to learn the job thoroughly; and so I stuck it out until I'd been there six months, and was fully experienced as a cutter.

I was then five months pregnant; but with another pram to buy and more baby clothes etc – well, we were a long way off buying our dream home. As Our Mam used to say,

'Ya' never want to plan owt'. Allus' say 'All being well.'

How wise she was.

Chapter Twelve

It seemed that the 'dream house' we'd planned to buy for so long was going to be just that – a 'dream house'. Never again would I make plans; or so I thought at the time.

But now I had to plan for this third baby. Again I started to knit and sew. I'd have to buy another pram, for we'd sold the previous one, but a former work mate sold me her large, navy, Silver Cross pram; an elegant affair fit for a Princess. Would we have a Princess, I wondered? Just our luck to have all boys, I thought mournfully.

But old lady Booth who lived a few doors away, told me I was lucky to have boys.

'The Queen 'ud envy you,' she told me, 'Having a boy every time. Anyway, it might be a girl.'

She was a dear old soul, this old lady, and gave me lots of advice about things; about cooking and dealing with kiddie's ailments, and what neighbours to beware of; for I was a trusting soul and could see good in everybody.

'When I was young none of the married women went out to work. We'd enough to do looking after our families, besides,' she went on, 'Whatever money yer' have coming in yer' learn to make do. To cut according to yer' cloth.' What wisdom; what a sensible old lady she was.

And so for the final four months of my pregnancy I kept myself busy. We knew we couldn't go on holiday that year, couldn't really afford it with another baby coming. Besides, I'd be too self-conscious about my lump, wearing thin summer dresses. I was painfully shy. So – I compromised. I made myself a Summer coat, creamy coloured, with raglan sleeves. The material only cost five bob a yard, so, with lining and buttons, I had a coat for just over a pound.

Up till now I had made the boys' overcoats and Jackie Coogan style caps; but now I decided I'd buy them a suit each; short trousers and jackets. They were a light tweed, both the same, and Oh my, didn't they look smart.

They were so proud of their first suits so, on the Sunday morning I took them down to the garden to show their Dad; and I was wearing my new coat, but feeling very conscious of my bulge. Oh happy days.

We'd no inkling then of the drama that was to come.

By this time my brother Harold had met and married a girl from an Agency Dating System. She was a sensible girl, small and neat and hard working. She was an Ilkestonian but had been living in London. They bought a bungalow at High Lane, West Hallam; but they never settled there, both had itchy feet, and after their first son John, was born, emigrated to Australia.

Marian, the shy, quiet one, was now in her teens and worked in a factory doing a very menial, easy job; but still she wouldn't mix with the other girls. The foreman treated her with scorn, which made her retreat more and more into her shell. And a few years later she was a patient at the Pastures Hospital for several years. Poor Marian, and all those other shy people like her, who never seem to live life to the full.

August came in with a blaze of sunshine that year, and my time was fast approaching. But I had developed an agonising backache, and when I walked up the street, would have to hold on to the wall for support, and seemed to lob on to my right side.

'It'll clear up when the baby's born,' I thought. But it didn't.

August 13th, and Dr Myers called to check up on me.

'In the morning my girl I want you to take 2 ounces of Castor Oil – in hot milk. You'll probably need me later in the day.'

GOSH – after I'd done as he told me next morning I felt

that I was losing everything I possessed. Most of the morning was spent on the lav. But it did the trick, and by four o'clock John was asking Stan Short from the top of the street, if he'd take me up to the Maternity Home in his car.

Again my husband was sent straight home. Husbands were not encouraged to be present at births at that time. Having a baby was a very private affair. The pain and unsightliness was something spared to the stronger sex. But – as Our Mam often said, 'If men had to goo' through it all thee wu'nt be so many babies born.' How often has that been said?

At 9.30 that evening my baby was born.

'You have a lovely daughter,' Nurse Elvira told me. She was a Spanish girl, very pleasant, very dedicated.

'A girl – are you sure?' I was so overjoyed, as John would be when he knew. 'We've not picked any girl's names,' I told her. John rang at 10 p.m. He'd made the call from a kiosk at the bottom of Bath Street, and was so relieved and overjoyed he'd left his pipe there, and had to retrieve it later, when he and a neighbour, Bernard Dawson, came back from the Rutland Hotel where they'd gone to wet the baby's head.

But things were not going well. For the next few days I was so weak I kept going into a faint, and felt at times that I was leaving this world. Matron told me I was being 'mardy'.

'After each child the after birth pains get worse,' she said.

'But I've never been afraid of pain,' I told her. 'I just feel ill all the time.' The Sister decided to call in Dr Myers. By then there was a huge lump below my right ribs.

'Looks like a strained muscle,' the Doctor said.

I still felt as if I was dying, and tried so hard to suckle my beautiful little daughter. I shed literally buckets of tears.

'You'll be alright when you get back home,' John tried to console me, and he regaled me with antics the boys had got up to.

Then I was home and all the neighbours small children

were lining up to inspect the new baby, exclaiming at the smallness of her fingers, and touching her silky, dark brown hair. We named her Christine Mary.

But when I took her for her first walk in the new pram, I only made it to the top of the street. I felt so faint I had to come back. The pain in my back was terrific, and the lump was getting bigger. I wept with frustration.

By the end of three weeks I decided to see the Doctor. It was Doctor Sudbury; Doctor Myers was out on call. Doctor Sudbury was noted for his bluntness. He took one good look at me, examined the lump on my side, then–

'Good God, woman – how long have you been like this?'
I told him.

'We'll have you up at the Hospital on Thursday. See what Hunt's got to say.' Mr Hunt I knew, was a surgeon. Heavens! What now?

So – Mam took care of the baby whilst I struggled up the hill to the hospital. It was an agony to walk, and after a half hour's probing by the surgeon and his assistant I was exhausted. How I got back home I'll never know.

The following week I had to go into Ilkeston General Hospital for tests. How to arrange for my family to be cared for was the problem. But a sister-in-law of Johns said the boys could go there for dinner each day. She and her husband kept a chip shop, and it was handy, being on the way home from school.

Mam said she'd take care of my six weeks' old baby. So – she prepared the bottom drawer of her dressing table for the baby to sleep in; it would save carting the crib around. Anyway, I'd probably only be in hospital for a few days. Little did I know.

I had to wean my baby quickly, but I wasn't sure what to do, so, on the advice of Old Lady Booth I went to see Miss Wood, at the Chemists on Bath Street. I told her my problem.

'Tight bands round your bust and plenty of Epsom Salts,' she told me. I shuddered. I was still remembering the 2 oz of Castor Oil.

Mam said she'd fetch the baby, and baby clothes. I was in too much pain to walk to Cotmanhay, a mile and a half away. John had an hour off work and took me to the hospital. That was in September.

What a predicament to be in. Two small boys and a baby a few weeks old, and here was I, powerless to take care of them; and John had to go to work – we needed the money.

For the next few days the nurses took samples of my urine every few hours, on the dot; and these samples were sent to Derbyshire Royal Infirmary to be analysed. What did they expect to find? I was mystified. I was usually so 'well up' on anything to do with the body.

One evening, when I'd been in hospital almost three weeks, John asked if he could speak to the Sister.

'Can you tell us what's wrong with my wife?'

Sister Webster smiled, then said two words, the second of which was 'Nephritis'. We were puzzled.

'It means diseased kidney', and then in a perfectly ordinary voice she told us. 'It will probably have to come out.' I was shocked. I was incredulous. Then, in scarcely above a whisper I said,

'But I shall die.'

Chapter Thirteen

After the initial shock had worn off, and I realised that my body would soon be functioning on just one kidney, I accepted the future with my usual stoical calm. I was a fatalist – what has to be will be. But I was also an intense realist – I wasn't going to let this crisis get me down.

I was frightened – believe me I was terribly afraid. I could not possibly see how I could live with just one kidney. But the Doctors were most reassuring as were the Sisters and nurses.

'You could live to be ninety,' they told me. I was then thirty-six years old.

The results of the urine tests came back from the analyst; the kidney was definitely not functioning, and so plans were made to operate in ten days time. It was the end of September.

Then the following day John came to see me, greatly agitated.

'It's your Mam – she's not been feeling well,' he told me. 'She says looking after the baby's too much for her.'

'But what are we going to do?' I asked him. 'You can't stay off work.' At that time we'd got about £20 in the Post Office bank.

'We'll think of something,' he tried to sooth me.

When Dr Myers could see how worried I was he told me,

'You go home for a week, Mother; try to get something sorted out.'

So, home I went, and once again had my three children around me. But although I was in constant pain I cleaned the house from top to bottom. If I died I wasn't going to leave a dirty house for the mourners to find.

Luckily the baby Christine was a good baby, didn't cry much and had taken well to bottle feeding.

But I was getting desperate about what we were going to do with her when I went into Hospital again.

Then John's sister Elsie came to see me and when she heard of our predicament, she soon offered to help.

'I'll take care of her. Don't worry yourself any more. Get someone to bring her crib up to our house.' She lived the other end of town, and they had a nine year old daughter, Freda.

Next day I got all the baby's things ready, and Elsie set off with the pram and my eternal thanks. Mr Woodhouse, who lived on the street and did a bit of carting took the crib for me. The boys would still be going to the sister-in-laws for their midday meal.

So I was able to go into Hospital on the Wednesday with a feeling of relief.

Thursday was Operation Day. My husband said a tight-lipped, tearful goodbye and I was left with my chaotic thoughts.

Would I come out of this alive, I wondered, or would my husband become a widower with three young children to care for?

I prayed and prayed as I had never prayed before; I didn't want to die, I had so much to live for. I had taken recent snapshots of the boys and even the new baby with me, and I wept over them and willed myself to come through it all alive.

Mrs Murphy in the next bed, who had had a Hysterectomy, tried to keep up my spirits, as did the Varicose Veins patient on the other side.

Then it was Thursday. No breakfast, no drinks, nothing. I was ravenous; I'd always enjoyed my food. But I'd make up for it I vowed. If I lived, that was.

I was dressed in my operation robe, which reminded me

of a shroud, and thick white socks were put on my legs. Then I was given the pre-med, and was soon in a relaxed state of euphoria. I took one last look at the snapshots of my children, through misty eyes. Mrs Murphy was watching me – her eyes were misty too. Then she said,

'We shall all pray for you. God bless ya' me' gel'.'

I was lifted on to the trolley and taken down the corridor and into the theatre. The Spinal Injection is something I'm not going to dwell on. Sufficient to say that although my body was soon numb to pain I was vaguely aware of what was going on; felt the occasional tug and movement of the Surgeon.

But I was also aware of a young, blond assistant who stood behind me, and from time to time mopped my forehead, and spoke reassuringly to me. I remember hanging tightly on to his thumb the whole time, even when I was wheeled down the corridor two and a half hours later.

Strong, gentle arms lifted me on to the bed, and soft voices soothed me. The bed was warm and I was soon in a dreamlike state. Later on I was vaguely aware of John sitting beside the bed, and a sister gently tapping my face. But all I wanted to do was sleep.

I was aware too, during the night of the soft hands and gentle voice of Sister Wrigley as she ministered to me, and now know why they call them 'angels'.

Six o'clock and I was being propped up on pillows, and a very welcome cup of tea was handed to me. I could see then that I had a Saline drip beside the bed, and it was connected to my wrist. But GOSH, wasn't I hungry?

Mrs Murphy and the varicose veins patients were smiling at me, and asking how I felt; and apart from a thick wadge of dressing at my right side I didn't feel too bad.

Soon an orderly was coming round with breakfast and I was given milky porridge.

'Can I have some bread, or toast or something?' I asked. 'I'm starving.' Nurse smiled at me.

'Can't give you solids until you've seen the Doctor.' Came the bed-pan round, the washing and talcuming, and medication and I could take stock of my surroundings.

There were several Hysterectomies, two Varicose veins; a woman with two black eyes and lots of bruises; she'd been brought in late, after the pubs had closed. And there was a frail elderly lady who was dying of Cancer.

Then the Doctors started on their rounds. Dr Sudbury examined me and I told him I was hungry.

'Take this bugger out,' he grinned at Sister, pointing to the Saline drip. 'Give her something to eat. D'you like a drink?' he asked me. I nodded.

'Yes – I like a Guinness.'

'Right – let her have a Guinness every night.'

I soon grew accustomed to the routine of hospital life, and made good progress. I was more determined than ever to get better quickly, so that I could look after my family; be a complete mother again.

On visiting days Elsie would bring the baby, pushing the large pram a good two miles from the other end of town. Sister Webster, who'd sadly lost her first child, would take my baby into the Staff room, then, ten minutes before visiting time was up, would bring her in to me. Elsie made sure she was spotlessly clean, and I never ceased to be grateful to her for her help.

By then it was time to say a tearful farewell to the boys as well, for they'd been waiting out in the corridor, and were allowed in for a few minutes.

One of the Varicose patients always wanted a bed-pan when visitors were there, and, behind closed curtains would put the pan on the floor and stand over it. Well – I leave you to imagine the sound it made. Then her voice would rise above all the chatter.

'Can you hear the chamber music?'

When it was one of the Hysterectomy's Wedding Anniversary, her husband brought in an iced, sponge cake to be divided among us all. We asked the nurses to pull the screens around them – just for a laugh. You can imagine the comments we called out to them.

Inevitably there was one patient who grumbled all the time; found fault with everything.

'I'm not used to these thick cups; I drink out of china at home. When I'm taking the waters at Buxton I'm treated like a lady.'

'Yer'd better ger'off back to Buxton then,' someone called.

Oh there were plenty of laughs during the month I stayed in Hospital, but above all, infinite kindness and gentleness.

Then, in the early part of October when Night Nurse came on duty, she told those of us who were awake,

'The Queen has had a son; it's just come through on the wireless.'

And so Prince Charles was born. A future heir to the throne.

Chapter Fourteen

It was the end of October, 1948 when I came out of hospital; still very weak, and minus a kidney. I had been in hospital seven weeks altogether, a huge chunk out of my life, or so I thought at that time. BUT – I was alive.

At first I just had the boys to see to; Elsie said she'd keep the baby, Christine, for another two weeks, until I felt a bit stronger. At first John shopped for me, at the weekends; the big shopping, and I did what housework I could, but still had to rest a lot.

When the two weeks was up and Elsie reluctantly handed the baby over to me, I felt so strange, even at changing a nappy. I'm sure Elsie would have kept the baby, if we'd said 'yes'; they'd grown so fond of her.

Gradually I got stronger but I knew it would be a long time before I felt my old self again; doing all my own housework, and shopping and my favourite pastime, gardening.

Then it was Christmas, a rather quiet affair this year. I'd made several soft toys for Christmas, and we'd secretly set aside a scooter each for the boys, with thick, rubber tyred wheels. We'd been paying a few shillings each week on them. John called at the shop for them late on Christmas Eve.

Before the children hung up their stockings John pretended he'd heard a noise up the chimney.

'He's here,' he told the boys, and he put his arm part way up the chimney. 'Got him,' he exclaimed and in his hand he clutched a ball of white fluff; a piece off Santa's beard. Young John and Ron were most impressed. It was as well they didn't know it was just a piece of cotton wool.

After the children were all in bed we sat and listened to the wireless. We'd not yet got around to buying a television set; much too expensive. Besides, television was a very new thing, on a par with refrigerators.

And so to bed.

Whilst it was still dark I was awakened by a strange sound, a soft thud-thud. I looked at the clock, 5.45. Still the sounds. I awakened John.

'I reckon there's someone outside – d'you think it's burglars?'

'Shouldn't think so – we've n'owt worth pinching.' He got out of bed, and went to the window. 'Eh up Else – just ya' look here,' he said.

I did, and there were two small boys, scootering away up and down the street. It was John and Ron.

'The young rascals,' John exclaimed, 'I never heard 'em get up, did you?' And he went downstairs to fetch them in. But we didn't get any more sleep that night.

It was the usual thing at that time for most children to have just one toy at Christmas, with a few sweets, maybe a Selection Box or a book. That was it. And they seemed satisfied. A bit different today, isn't it? I wonder if they are any happier with today's computers, and all the paraphernalia that goes with them?

Christmas was such a happy time that year; our little family was complete – two fine sons and now a daughter. I was getting stronger every day, and my husband was so helpful. He'd bath both the boys at night, in the tin bath in front of the fire, whilst I got the baby ready for bed. Then it would be cocoa for us all, and after the boys were in bed we'd sit and listen to a play on the wireless, and I'd thank God for another day nearer complete health.

Spring was with us again, and time to start planning for the garden. In the evening we'd all go down there until it was dark, and I'd prick out the seedlings into trays whilst the baby looked on contentedly from her pram, and the boys tended their own little patch. John would be digging, and setting, and would look across at us from time to time, a happy smile on his face.

Those gardens have now all disappeared with the development of the housing estate at the rear of Springfield Gardens, right down to the canal side.

We decided we'd take the children to the seaside that Summer, so we asked Aunt Ethel if we could again rent the bungalow at Ingoldmells. Christine, the baby, would then be a year old. By this time we had acquired a puppy, a black, lurcher type dog; so we'd take him too. We called him Flash, and he was true to his name, was like a streak of black lightning.

We arranged with a man who lived nearby to go in his car. He would bring other holiday makers back with him; a regular shuttle service. That way we could take a push chair with us, and lots of foodstuff, as well as clothes, sheets and towels etc. This time I took a new bathing suit and it HADN'T got a padded bra – I'd learned my lesson.

Christine was walking by then, halting steps on her little, podgy legs, and the boys were enchanted with her, and watched over her as she built sand castles with them. And we all splashed about in the waves and had loads of fun. In the mornings, while the children still slept John and I would take Flash for a walk along the beach, and he'd pick up huge pieces of driftwood, and we'd run back with him like a couple of kids.

We made friends with another family; he was a policeman on holiday, and they had two boys. Some days we'd all pile into his car, an estate model, and we'd drive into the country or up to Mablethorpe.

'Cor Dad, can we have a car?' the boys asked after one such drive.

Those holidays at Aunty's bungalow were truly wonderful times, and we went there for several years. Sadly, in 1952 with the great tidal wave which swept the East Coast the wooden structure was lifted bodily off its moorings, over the dyke and into Billy Butlin's holiday camp. It was a sorry sight along that coast; streets and roads and farmland flooded to a depth of several feet.

At the Haven where Aunty's bungalow was, most of the wooden buildings were piled up in a tangled mass of wreckage, and when Uncle Will went down after the floods had subsided he found that lots of things had been stolen, a large tool box amongst them. All they got for the loss of their holiday home was £50, either from Insurance or Government compensation; I'm not sure which.

12 Railway coach holiday near Ambergate

The following year we holidayed much nearer home. We hired a railway coach beside the River Derwent at Ambergate. Two compartments opened up formed the living-room-cum-kitchen, and the corridor led to other compartments which formed the bedrooms. It was so compact, so cosy, and in the morning we could pull back the bedroom curtains and see ducks and swans basking in the early sun on the river banks right below us.

13 (Left to Right) John, Christine and Ron, in front of the
dreaded wash-house in Slade Street!

Whilst I prepared breakfast John and the boys, towels
slung across shoulders would walk across the field to a
spring, which ran into a trough, and wash in the clear, cold
water. The grass around the holiday coaches had been cut,
and the children spent many happy hours tossing the hay
and hiding in it.

One day we walked up the steep hill to Crich, and
climbed to the top of Crich stand where we could see into
several counties. Another day we walked to Cromford, by
the road pointing out to the boys ants and other
creepy-crawlies which inhabited the stone walls. Then we
walked back through Cromford Meadows and along the
canal as far as The Derwent Hotel, when we were in sight of
our holiday home.

Yet another time we walked up the steep hill to
Alderwasley, pronounced Allersley, or so I later learned
from an old fella leaning on a stone wall, and we came to the
Malt Shovel and looked down at Wirksworth in the mist
below us; and of course we refreshed ourselves at the pub,
for we had a long walk back downhill. We took sandwiches

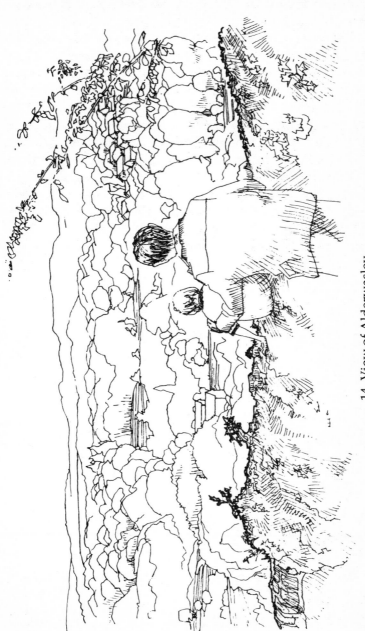

14 View of Alderwasley

on these long hikes, but were all ravenous when we got back home.

On these roads we only occasionally saw a car; plenty of horses from the farms. Every thing was so much slower then, more restful; no jumping out of the way of traffic. And the hire of the holiday coach was only £4 for the week. A neighbour took us there and back in his car for £2.10s. What a cheap holiday that was, but oh! how we enjoyed it.

When I think of today's prices, £80 to £100 for a caravan for a week, then the cost of bus or train fares; and if you take your own car with petrol at around £2 a gallon, then I look back at that holiday beside the Derwent, it seems incredible that prices can change so drastically. But we all voted that our cheap holiday at Ambergate, by the river, was one of the best we'd ever had.

Chapter Fifteen

Isn't it strange how one thing leads to another? When young John was nine years old and at Gladstone Junior School, he said he'd like to learn to play the piano so I, always eager to encourage young talent bought a second hand Charles Foulds piano for £20.

One of my husband's mates at Shipley Colliery, a Mr Stirland, taught pianoforte in his spare time, so John went there for lessons each week. Now I'd always been keen to learn to play so decided I'd have lessons as well. The cost – half a crown an hour.

Young John plodded along and seemed to be doing quite well, and easily passed his first exam at Nottingham. But he soon lost interest with the classical pieces he was expected to play, and begged to finish his lessons.

But I played on, although I never did work up much speed. I suppose at nearing forty my fingers had stiffened up.

Mr Stirland's wife, I discovered, was an old school friend from Junior School days. She invited me to join the Cotmanhay Townswomen's Guild, of which she was a member, and which had a flourishing choir. I told John about it.

'Yes, of course you can go – It's only one night a week. I can manage the kids for one night'. So, full of enthusiasm I joined the Guild, and the choir, singing second soprano.

Now I'm no Joan Sutherland but I could keep in tune, and could read the music; and with all the deep breathing it entailed I was soon feeling as fit as a fiddle.

John would meet my bus home, after he'd put the

children to bed, and he'd have a bag with a couple of basins in it, and we'd call at the chip shop. Chips were 2p and 3p a portion, and fried fish, 8p. Unbelievable but true. And how I'd enjoy my supper that night, for the singing had made me 'fair famished' to use an old Ilkeston saying.

We were practising The Cloud, to sing at a festival at the Albert Hall at Nottingham.

Came the great day and I felt very nervous; my old shyness returning, and when I saw we were up against fifteen other choirs, felt more nervous than ever. But we had a good, confident conductor, a Miss Wheatley, and we did everything just right, breathing at the right time and with the correct intonation in every word. And we won.

We were all so elated, and when our bus reached Bath Street and my bus stop I ran the rest of the way home to tell John the good news. Then of course next day I had to go over to Mam's to tell her as well.

Then there was Aunt Ethel at Nottingham to write to. Whatever I did I always kept her informed, as I did for the rest of her life, and she lived to be 94. She always was my great confidante and how I missed the old dear when she died.

I was so full of enthusiasm for anything I did at that time, and would wake every morning almost bursting with joy at just being alive.

We sang at several Music Festivals during that year, at Lincoln, Selston, Alfreton, and would often entertain Old People's clubs singing the old favourites.

Then one day Mrs Roach, who was leader of the Drama Group, asked me if I'd act in a mime. It was called 'Chelsea China', and I was to act the male part. So, out of an old blue velvet cape Mrs Roach gave me I made an 18th Century swallow tailed jacket. With it I wore pink silk knee breeches, white stockings with black buckled shoes, and a friend loaned me a cravat of Honiton lace, and wrist ruffles to match.

My lady partner wore a pink crinoline dress, with a voluminous skirt, and when the mime started, to the accompaniment of the music in an 18th Century Drawing Room, we were poised over a chess table. We were brought to life by the music, then the lights would gradually change as a Gavotte was played, and we danced with, oh – so much decorum. We received a great ovation and were asked to repeat 'Chelsea China' at lots of other concerts.

Later on Mrs Roach, whose son Bill is Kenneth Barlow of Coronation Street fame, asked me if I could run a stall at the Guild's Spring Fair. I thought for a while – cakes – white elephant stall – I wasn't too keen. Then suddenly –

'How about a Gypsy Fortune Teller?' I suggested.

'Why that's great, could you do it?' she asked.

So that's how I became Madame Elsa Romanina. That's what the Zodiac card told the public outside my tent, and I lived the part.

I wore a red, spotted kerchief on my head, with huge curtain rings for earings, and a voluminous black silk skirt, braided round the bottom. My crystal ball was a gold fish bowl, and in between readings I'd puff cigarette smoke inside, to make it look mysterious. Not being much used to smoking it's a wonder I didn't choke to death.

I made pounds for Guild funds with that little act, and was in great demand at Galas and Coffee evenings. But with all the swotting up it entailed, learning about what the lines on the palms signified, learning to read the cards, and the great excitement of the day itself, well – I could hardly sleep at nights.

I well remember one Summer Fete in the Vicarage gardens at Cotmanhay Parish Church. I was given a tent to myself, in a corner with the usual queue forming outside. Inside, the light was dim, and I must have looked mysterious sitting there, my crystal ball beside me, swirling with vapour inside; my face and hands tanned to a 'gypsy brown'. My clients came and went, seemingly satisfied, for I knew a great deal about their family life, having lived among them before I married. But with my camouflage it seemed that not many recognised me; so I could spin them a yarn with a great degree of accuracy.

15 Gypsy Fortune Teller at Vicarage

Then, in came a lady I'd not seen before. She was smart, slim and attractive. I studied her palms.

'My word – we have a passionate nature here,' I told her, as I studied the well raised Mounts of Venus at the base of her thumbs which is supposed to denote a loving and passionate personality. Her face gave nothing away at all; not like some of my clients who rattled away as soon as they entered the tent, and told me lots before I could even speak.

I spun the usual yarn to this lady, but couldn't resist adding,

'I guess your husband is pleased to have such a passionate lady for his wife.' She smiled an enigmatic smile, her face as inscrutable as the Sphinx, put her half crown on the plate and went outside.

One of the helpers popped her head inside the tent. 'Could you cut it a bit shorter? Stalls are nearly empty and you've still got a queue outside.' So, I gave them a bit less patter until the last client had gone, then added up the afternoon's takings which came to six or seven pounds. A lot at that time for a one man effort.

'There's tea waiting at the Vicarage. Vicar's out here, he wants to thank you,' a voice called. So – collecting my takings I went outside into the bright glare of sunshine; and there stood the benevolent gentleman with a smile lighting up his face. The proceeds from the other stalls MUST have been good. I'd not met this Vicar before and was surprised that he looked so young. He shook my hand warmly.

'Thank you so much Madame Elsa,' he told me, 'Whatever would we do without you ladies? Oh – and may I introduce my wife?' as a slim, attractive lady came over to join us.

Yes – you've guessed – it was the lady with the passionate palms. I was glad of my dark makeup, which helped to hide my blushes.

One Summer, all the Townwomen's Guilds in Derbyshire got together to put on a glorious pageant of dancing through the ages. The venue was to be Swanwick Hayes, an imposing mansion set above lovely, terraced lawns, an ideal setting for such an historical event.

I was one of eight ladies chosen from our Guild to do a Saxon dance – we formed two quartettes. But I had to take a man's role. The dress was the easiest part. One sugar sack with a hole at the top for my head, and at each side for my arms. A cord around my waist and flat rope sandals for my feet, with thongs around my legs up to my knees. My hair was shoulder length, just right, but I had to wear a beard, stuck on in tufts with gum, but oh gosh – didn't it take some removing?

16 Elegantly cross-gartered as a Saxon man (extreme left!) at the Swanwick pageant

The ladies wore long, hopsack, baggy dresses, and had white cloth draped around their head and shoulders; a kind of Wimple. The dance was slow and ponderous, and performed to the music of a flute.

The day was perfect when we arrived at Swanwick, and we were soon walking about the Cypress landscaped gardens in full dress. But I felt most dowdy when we came upon a group of Elizabethan ladies surrounding their Queen, resplendent in the gorgeous dress of that period, and the gardens were a perfect foil to them.

As the time for the start of the pageant approached the sky darkened. Then all at once the rain came down; a typical English, Summer's day; and so we all piled into a large, wooden building to start our pageant of Dance.

But catastrophies like this never daunted the ladies of the Townswomen's Guilds. We were a tough lot. For us, like all other members of the acting fraternity, the show had to go on.

Chapter Sixteen

1958 was a truly momentous year for us. My husband decided to leave the colliery. With the opening of a drift mine and all the extra work it entailed, the pressure had piled up, and he'd quite literally bring his work home with him. As he confided to a friend later,

'I found I was snapping at the kids for the least little thing, and I wasn't going to have that.' And so he went back to Stanton, on the Concrete Section.

The boys were doing well at school; young John began to shine in Art, but Ron went more for the practical things, and especially sport.

Christine was at Chaucer Infant's School, so I decided I'd try for another part time job. I found one, as a cutter at Fletcher's factory, just over the wall from where we lived. I was to cut out silk this time, for ladies underwear, using rather formidable electric cutters. But – it WAS a job, and I was able to start saving, for we were determined to go to the seaside again that year.

I worked until four o'clock, and Christine would come straight from school to meet me, with her little sweetheart Christopher. He lived two doors away from us, and every morning he'd be waiting for her by the back door in the entry. Oh it was good to see the devotion of those two.

The boys stayed for school dinners, and I'd have their tea waiting for them when they got home. I was determined I wasn't going to have them roaming the streets until I finished work. A child needs a mother to be there at home, if he or she is going to grow up with a feeling of security, a well balanced personality. This is the way I see it. I could be wrong.

That Summer we were lucky enough to find a bungalow at Mablethorpe, a plain, brick structure with one large bedroom, a living room and tiny kitchen. It was at the top of Golf Road, which led straight down to the sands.

When we arrived, again by train and a short bus ride the owner had lit a fire, and was waiting to greet us, AND to collect the rent, which was about £8. He welcomed us like long lost relatives, made a fuss of the dog, and that was the last we saw of him.

The beds were hard, the furniture had seen much better days, and we only had a hot-plate on which to cook, but at least we couldn't spoil anything. It was very basic, but we had a 'whale' of a time. Early morning walks with Flash, finishing up at a beach hut drinking mugs of hot tea, and spending whole days on the sands.

We went there for many years after that, always to the same brick bungalow, and always the same chappie to

17 Kirk Hallam Estate

greet us, with a coal fire. Those holidays with the children were the best we ever had, carefree and full of laughter.

But back home again I was still feeling the urge to get away from the dark, terraced house in the back street where we lived. I felt stifled, and so on edge all the time, and John was as eager to leave as I was.

So, each week I scanned the pages of The Advertiser for a suitable swop.

There was a large Council Estate being built at Kirk Hallam where once was rolling green pastures, running down to the Stanton works. We liked the look of those houses, and it would be so handy for where John worked. Then one day, during October there was an ad in the paper, 'Wanted to exchange, three bedroomed Council house for one in centre of town.' And so with great trepidation we answered the advert.

Unbelievably we got an answer to our letter and arranged for the other people to view our house. But surely nobody in their right mind would want to leave a nice house to come into this poky little place? We weren't very hopeful.

The young couple came round to see us, seemed to like what they saw, and the girl said she'd be able to see more of her mother who lived near to us. And so we both applied for the exchange, but knew it would take quite a while, having to wait for the next Council Meeting.

On the Sunday we went up to look at the house at Kirk Hallam. It was pouring with rain; not a very good omen I thought. But the house with its large L shaped living room, with windows at either end, three bedrooms and a bathroom, and a separate toilet – well – it was like a palace to us, compared with our humble little place. There was a good sized kitchen, and an outhouse, also a large garden at the back, although it was sadly neglected. But – we liked the house and decided we could soon lick the garden into shape.

In the meantime the boys were practising a school play – Wind In The Willows. Young John was chosen to be Rat, and Ron was one of the rabbits. Mothers were expected to make the clothes, so I was kept busy. For John's tail I stuffed a long stocking, tapering the end to a point. A brown Balaclava helmet provided his headress, but the whiskers proved difficult until I had the bright idea of plucking the bristles off my yard brush. The rabbit's dress was easier; skin fitting stockinette for the body, with long felt ears on either side of the light brown Balaclava helmet.

That play was a great success, as was Richard The Lionheart. John played the lead in that one, and I used an old, white sheet for his uniform, with a large, felt red cross blazening the front, and the helmet coming around the shoulders knitted in thick grey wool. The enthusiasm with which he played the part was very evident when he disappeared over the back of the stage. That raised a laugh I can tell you, but, thankfully he wasn't hurt.

Then, just when we'd almost forgotten it the letter from the Council came. 'Your Council House exchange approved. Moving date December 30th.' Gosh – that was only four days after Christmas. I leave you to guess at all the preparation that went on during that month, but what a great feeling of elation to know that we'd soon be leaving this drab little house, in this dead end of a back street.

But first I had the boys' school parties to plan for. They were now both at Gladstone School, and both wanted to take trifles. Other Mothers would provide cakes and sandwiches. So – I got two of my largest glass dishes – both the same size to prevent any squabbling, and made two super trifles. I'd promised to help lay the tables, so I carefully carried the trifles myself.

The party was to be in the school hall, and what a picture the tables looked, absolutely ladened with goodies. And afterwards everything was cleared away, and rows of forms placed across the hall, facing the stage, for we were going to have an impromptu entertainment afterwards.

Greatly daring I, and a Mrs Fell went on to the stage and started the boys singing carols. Then we sang Rudolph The

Red Nosed Reindeer, and that really raised the roof. It was a super party and one I've never forgotten.

Then it was Christmas proper, but how busy we were, scrounging large boxes, tea chests, anything that would hold our belongings. Everything not in immediate use we would pack away. The furniture and bedding would have to be 'stoved' a term we used for the fumigation process the Council insisted on.

December the 30th dawned bright and clear – a lovely day. Then the removal men were there, and the boys wanted to help, carrying all the small items. A sack containing our clothes, towels and soft ware etc. was put in last, and that was the only item not to be 'stoved', that and a bag containing sandwiches and a flask. John had gone to work; his job was important and couldn't be left.

So there we were on a bright, sunny day at the end of December sitting on a large sack in the middle of the living room floor, eating sandwiches al-fresco style and surveying our new domain. To the children it was a great adventure, but to me it was like starting life all over again. I was already planning what colour I'd use for each room, for I planned to do the decorating myself. Well I would have all day on my own and I loved painting and paper-hanging.

When John came home from work it was already dark, and he pushed his bike up the wrong drive, a few houses below.

'I could see a strange woman at th' kitchen sink. I did feel daft,' he told us. Thankfully, we'd got all the furniture in place and I'd got curtains at the windows, and I'd even managed to cook a hot meal.

After the children were in bed we sat and made plans. Could we afford a carpet square for the living room; how much would linoleum cost for the bedrooms? Could we manage to build our own greenhouse? And I kept looking round our large, comfortable living room, and made excuses to keep going into the kitchen, to admire that too.

And later we sat and watched the television, which we could now afford, and John contentedly puffed at his pipe and looked across at me from time to time, and the dog, Flash lay stretched out across our feet, a picture of perfect harmony.

'Are ya' happy Else?' John asked. I nodded. I felt too full to speak, but our eyes spoke volumes to each other, full of promises to 'love and cherish as long as we both should live'. Another era of our life had begun.

What did the forthcoming years have in store for us, we wondered? One thing was for sure – whatever the future held, we'd face it together.